KNOWLEDGE ENCYCLOPEDIA

HUMAN BODY
SKELETAL & MUSCULAR SYSTEM

© Wonder House Books 2024

All rights reserved. No part of this book may be reproduced or transmitted in any form by any means, electronic or mechanical, including photocopying and recording, or by any information storage and retrieval system except as may be expressly permitted in writing by the publisher.

(An imprint of Prakash Books)

contact@wonderhousebooks.com

Disclaimer: The information contained in this encyclopedia has been collated with inputs from subject experts. All information contained herein is true to the best of the Publisher's knowledge.

ISBN : 9789389931242

Table of Contents

The Bones that Make Us	3
Protecting the Brain: The Skull	4–5
Stiffening the Back: The Vertebral Column	6–7
At the Heart of It: Shoulders and Ribs	8–9
Inside Your Bones	10–11
The Bones that Keep Us Going	12–13
In Your Hands and Feet	14–15
Some Very Hip Bones	16
Helping You Move: Skeletal Joints	17
How Joints Work	18–19
Breaking Point: Bone Fractures	20
Moving Our Bodies: Muscles and Tendons	21
The Muscles We Can Control	22
The Muscles We Cannot Control	23
How Muscles Work	24–25
Keeping the Heart Going	26
Exercise in Moderation	27
Getting Older	28–29
Osteoporosis	30
Muscular Diseases	31
Word Check	32

THE BONES THAT MAKE US

When you look into a mirror, you see the person that your bones and muscles made you. You might notice that you are tall or short, stocky or gangly. In the long course of evolution, bodies needed to adapt to protect themselves better and become stronger, faster and more agile. Muscles came first. You see muscles in animals as simple as nematodes. They help them move, find food and mate with partners. They also help digest food.

Bones helped create a stiff **endoskeleton** to which the muscles and other organs could attach. Other creatures, like insects and clams have **exoskeletons**, which are hard coverings outside their bodies. But exoskeletons do not give them the freedom of movement of limbs that our bones give us. The earliest 'bones' were actually made of cartilage, and then animals evolved to add mineral deposits of calcium phosphate to make them harder.

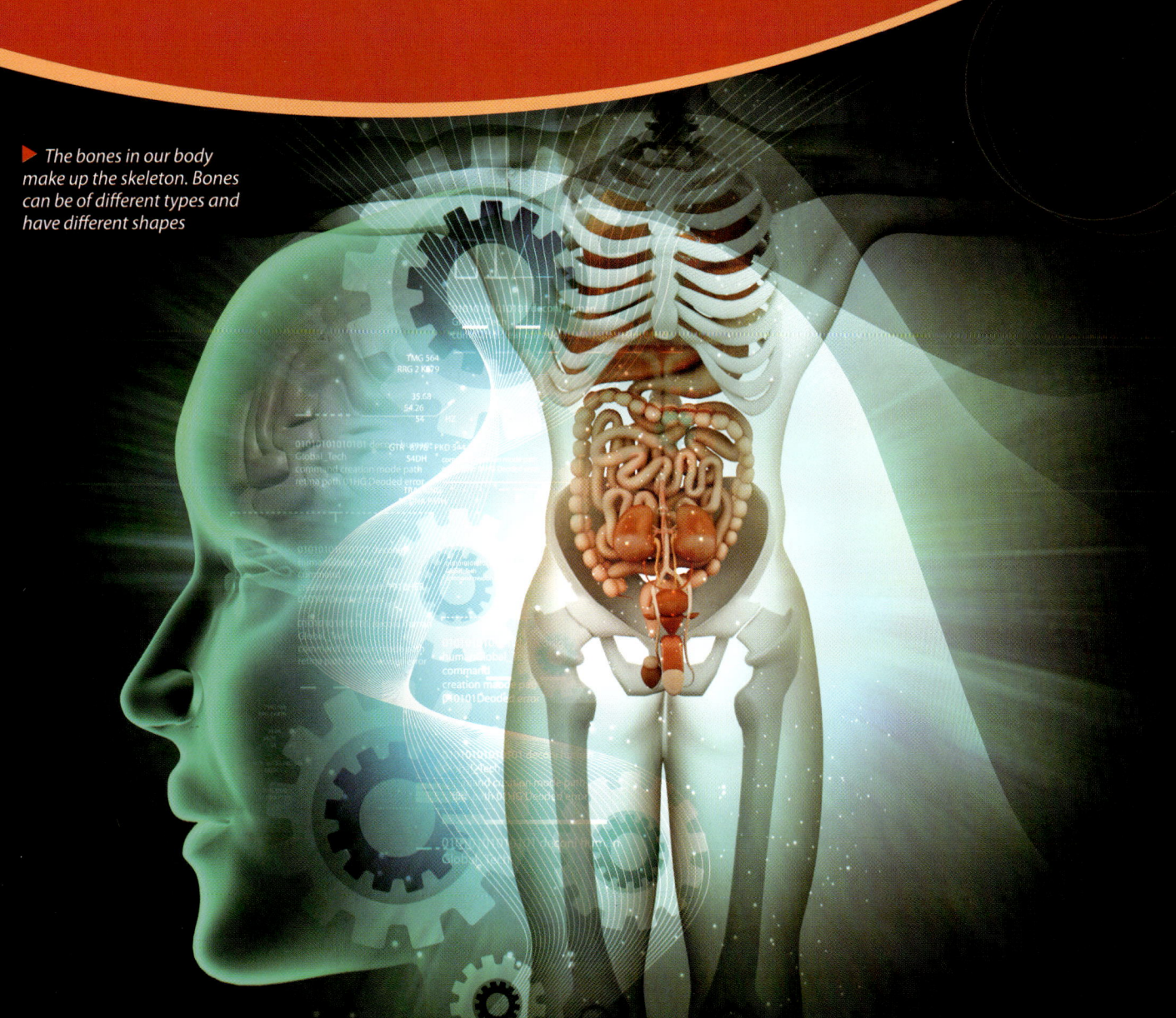

▶ The bones in our body make up the skeleton. Bones can be of different types and have different shapes

Protecting the Brain: The Skull

The skull has fascinated people from the beginning of time. It is a symbol of death and danger in many cultures. This could be attributed to the fact that the brain and the head are considered to be representative of a person. Brain damage can seriously impair one's life, and the functioning of any and all other parts of the body.

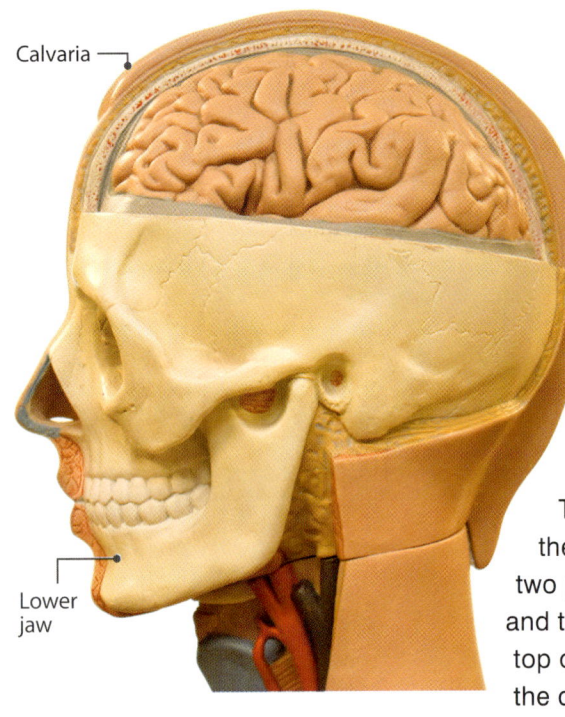

Calvaria

Lower jaw

The Brainbox

Human life wouldn't be the same without the skull. It protects the brain and the organs of the face, like the eyes, nose, inner ear and mouth. It is harder than most bones, so if you have a bad fall, your skull does not fracture easily.

The skull, also known as the cranium, is made of two parts—the brainbox, and the facial bones. The top of the skull is called the calvaria, its sides are called temples, while the bottom is called the base. Large plate-like bones enclose the brain. They are the frontal bone (the forehead), a pair of parietal bones (the back of your head), a pair of temporal bones (sides) and the occipital bone (the back of your neck). They correspond to the lobes of the cerebrum.

The temporal bone has a hole to let in the ear canal and the mandibular fossa, into which the lower jaw fits. The occipital bone has a large hole in it, through which the spinal cord passes from the brain to the body. The sphenoid makes the floor of the brain box. It is full of small holes to let in cranial nerves and arteries and let veins out. The last is the ethmoid bone, which also makes the roof and septum of the nasal cavity.

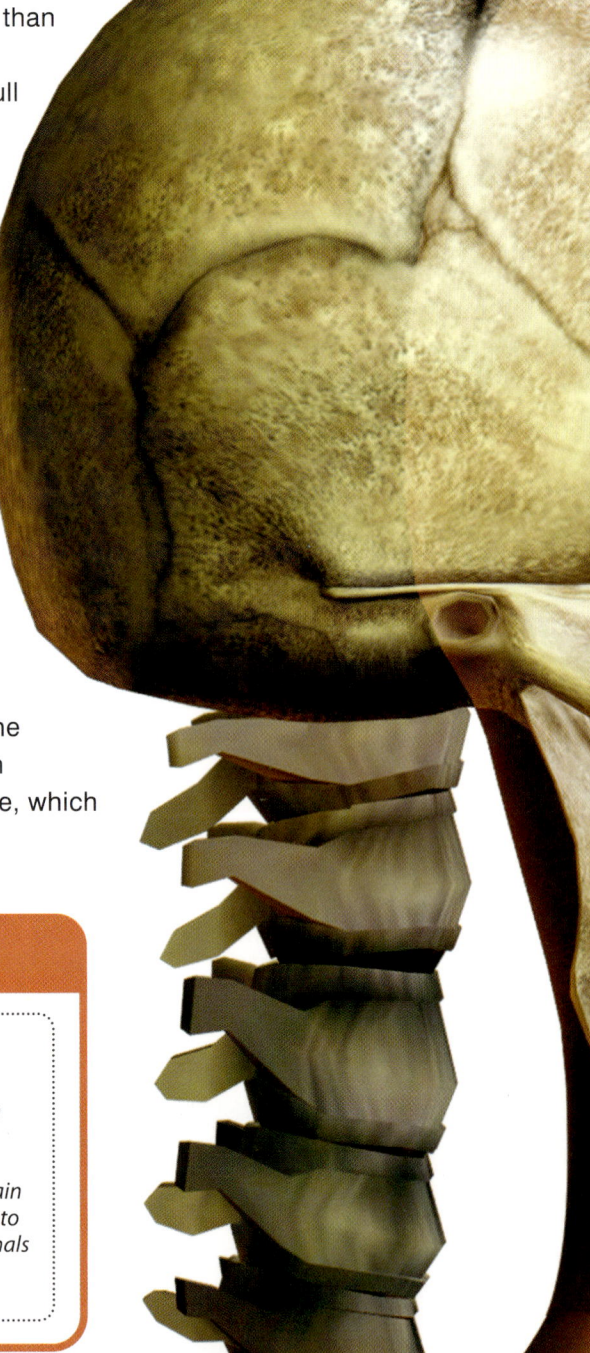

In Real Life

The human brainbox (in proportion to the rest of the body) is among the largest in the animal kingdom. It has to be, for it evolved to have a brain that is also the largest (in proportion to the body). The brain takes up over two-thirds of the skull.

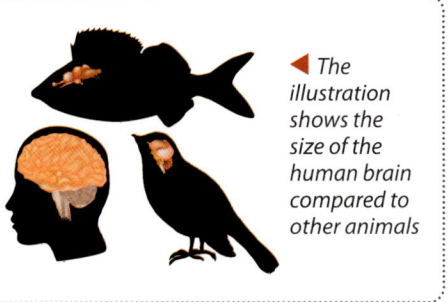

◂ The illustration shows the size of the human brain compared to other animals

HUMAN BODY — SKELETAL & MUSCULAR SYSTEM

⭐ Incredible Individuals

Have you seen someone in a plaster cast? They might have needed it because of an injury that broke their bones. This technique of using plaster to grip broken bones in a plaster cast was invented by a Dutch army doctor named Antonius Mathijsen in 1851. He realised that gypsum plaster, when mixed with water, would set very quickly, keeping bones in place.

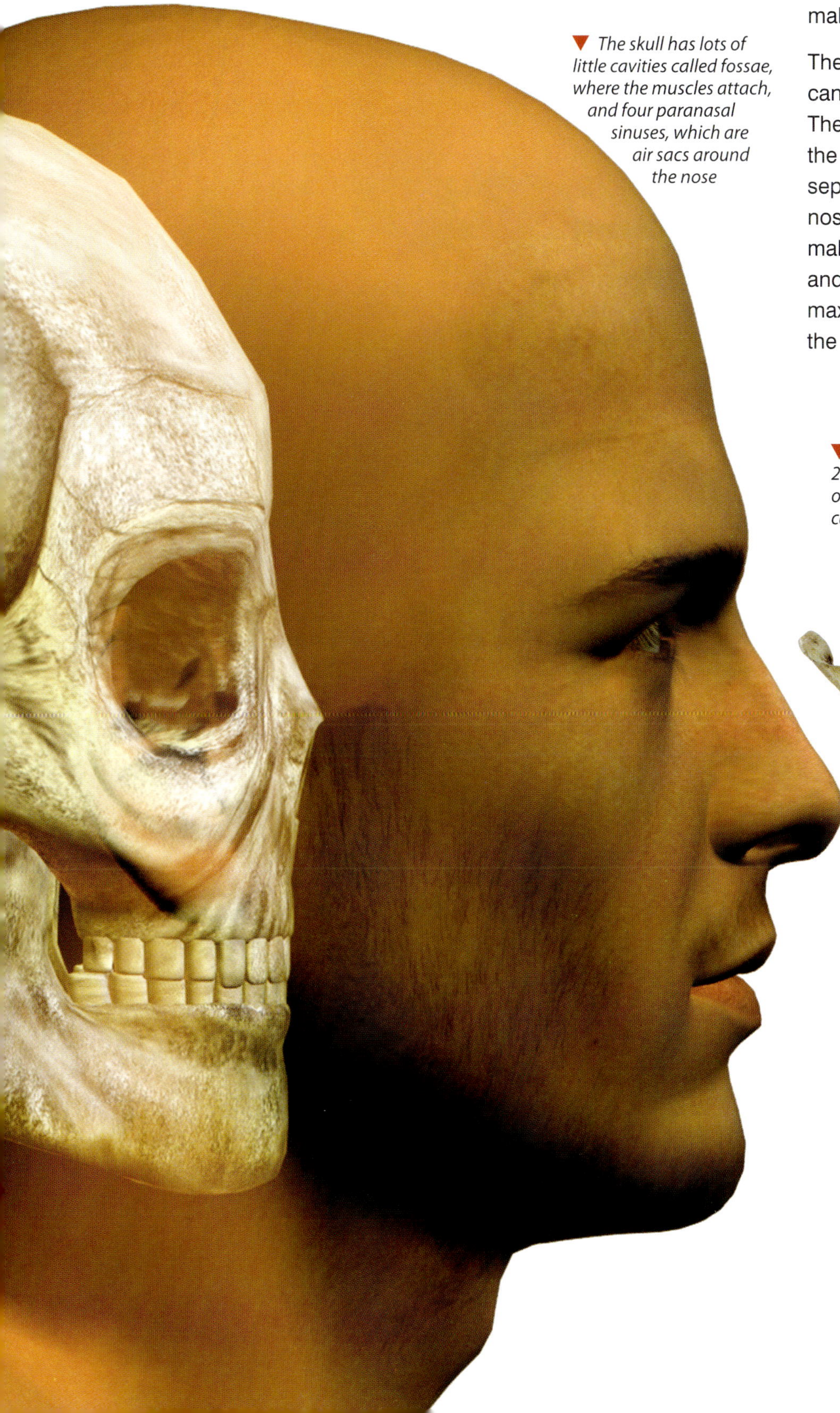

▼ *The skull has lots of little cavities called fossae, where the muscles attach, and four paranasal sinuses, which are air sacs around the nose*

Eyes and Nose

Your eyes sit in two cavities in the skull called the **orbit**. The frontal bone makes up the upper half of both the orbits. Your cheekbones (zygomatic bones) make up its outer sides. The optic nerve passes through the sphenoid in their back. The tiny lacrimal bones, and parts of the ethmoid, make up the inner sides. The **maxilla** makes up its floor.

The bony part of the nose that you can touch is made of the nasal bones. The single vomer and the ethmoid make the septum, which divides the nostrils. The septal cartilage, which makes your visible nose, attaches to the ethmoid. The palate makes both the floor of the nasal cavity and the roof of the mouth. It is made by the maxilla, and a small pair of bones called the palatines.

▼ *Your skull has 22 bones, of which only the lower jaw can move*

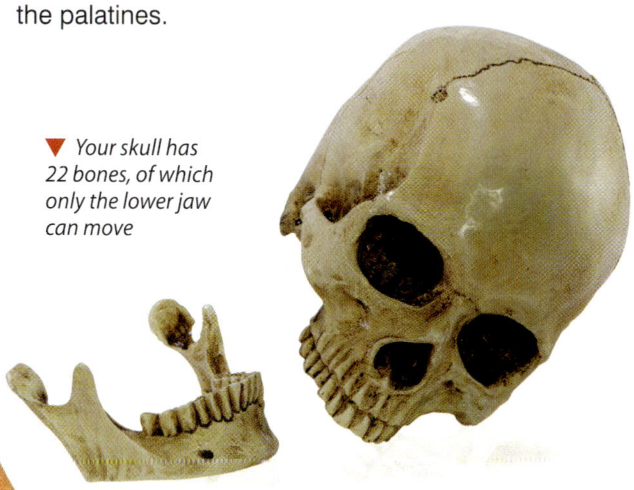

The Mouth

Your mouth is made of the jaws and the palate. The jaws contain your teeth. There are 24 teeth in children (milk teeth) and 32 teeth in adults. Your upper jaw is called the maxilla, which is actually a pair of bones joined together. The lower jaw is called the **mandible**. It is attached to the temporal bones on both sides of the mouth. The hyoid is a special bone, which is not attached to any other bones. It is behind the mandible and the tongue attaches to it.

Stiffening the Back
The Vertebral Column

◀ Let's take a look at the vertebra

The vertebral column, also called the spine, divides the animal kingdom into two—those without it (invertebrates) and those with it (vertebrates). Fish, amphibians, reptiles, birds and mammals are vertebrates, with a bony spine. In some fish (like sharks and rays) the spine, like the rest of the skeletal system, is made of cartilage. It develops from the notochord, a stiff rod-like organ in the embryo.

Spine

The spine is made of 33 bones called vertebrae (singular: **vertebra**). It protects the spinal cord, and provides an anchor for the ribs, the shoulders and the hips. It also helps you flex your body in many ways, so you can run around and play with ease.

The spine has five regions. As you grow, the vertebrae of the sacrum merge into each other to form a single bone which becomes part of the hip. The four tail vertebrae also merge to form the tiny coccyx, which curves inwards. Animals with tails have many more vertebrae in them.

In Real Life

Sometimes the gel-like part of the intervertebral disc gets crushed and comes out of the spine. This is called a slipped disc. It causes a lot of pain.

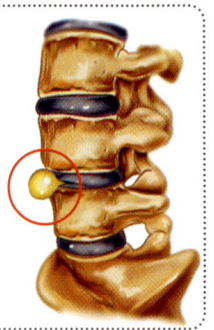

▶ An illustration of slipped disc with the problem area circled

Region	Type of Vertebrae	Number	Names of Vertebrae	Attaches to
Neck	Cervical	7	C1–C7	–
Upper Back	Thoracic	12	T1–T12	The ribs
Lower Back	Lumbar	5	L1–L5	–
Hip	Sacral	5	–	The hip bones
Tail (Coccyx)	Coccygeal	4	–	–

HUMAN BODY | SKELETAL & MUSCULAR SYSTEM

 # Vertebra

Each vertebra has three parts—a body, the vertebral arch and many processes. Between the bodies of two vertebrae are **intervertebral discs,** made of cartilage. The outer part of each is fibrous, while the inner part is jelly-like. These discs act as cushions when the vertebrae bend backwards or forwards, so that their bodies do not rub against each other. The vertebral arch extends in two arms that meet behind the vertebral foramen. The foramina of all the vertebra form a tube-like canal, through which the spinal cord passes.

Finally, the processes act as places where skeletal muscles attach. Vertebrae in different regions of the spine have different processes. The spinous process sticks out of each vertebra and points downwards. This stops you from twisting yourself too much and dislocating your spinal cord. The gaps between the vertebra are also spaces from which the spinal nerves pass from the spinal cord to various parts of the body.

▲ The segmentation of the spine gives your body incredible flexibility

◀ The S-shape of the spinal cord allows us to walk and run

 # Regional Vertebrae

Cervical vertebra has extra foramina, through which the arteries to the brain pass. The first of them (C1), is called atlas. It bears the weight of the skull. Its body is hollow. The second (C2), is called axis. Its body has a pivot called the dens, which fits into the hollow of atlas. This is what lets you turn your neck around.

▼ The diagram shows the five regions of the spine

The thoracic vertebra has processes to the side called transverse processes. Both they and the vertebral arch have dimples on both sides called facets. Here is where the ribs attach. Lumbar vertebrae have additional processes called articular processes, where muscles can attach. The fused arches of the sacral vertebrae make up an ear-like surface, to which the hip bones attach.

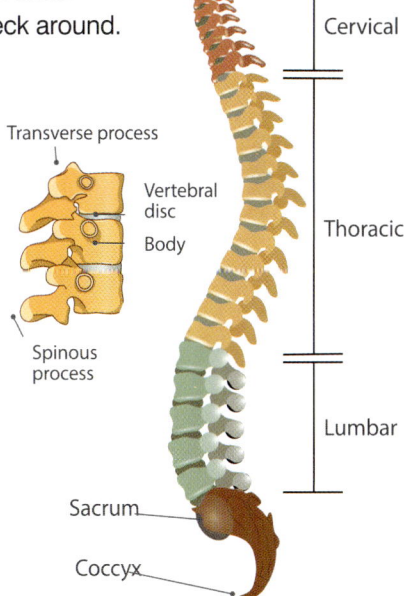

Transverse process
Vertebral disc
Body
Spinous process

Cervical
Thoracic
Lumbar
Sacrum
Coccyx

Isn't It Amazing!

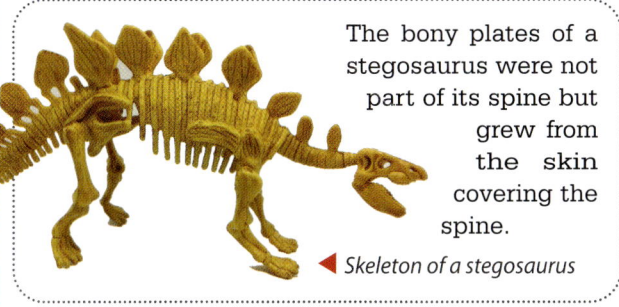

The bony plates of a stegosaurus were not part of its spine but grew from the skin covering the spine.

◀ Skeleton of a stegosaurus

At the Heart of It
Shoulders and Ribs

Your chest has two of the most important organs of your body, your lungs and your heart. As we evolved, our skeleton developed a tough protective cover for them—the ribcage or **thoracic basket**. It has your ribs, as well as the breastbone or **sternum**, which protects your heart and lungs from the front. The ribs end in the 12 thoracic vertebrae of the spine.

The top of the ribcage is covered by your collarbones, or clavicles, while the back is covered by the shoulder blades, or scapulae. These two make up the **pectoral girdle**, which allows you to move your arms and shrug your shoulders.

Pectoral Girdle

The clavicle is the easiest bone to figure out. You can feel it starting from the base of the neck to the beginning of the arms. The two clavicles make movable **joints** with the breastbone, so you can move your arms forward or back. When you move your forearms back, you can feel your shoulder blades.

Three powerful muscles attach to the pectoral girdle. The levator scapulae attaches it to the base of the skull and the cervical vertebrae. The two rhomboid muscles (major and minor) attach it to the thoracic vertebrae. Together, they allow the shoulder to bear a great amount of weight, whether on the back or the front.

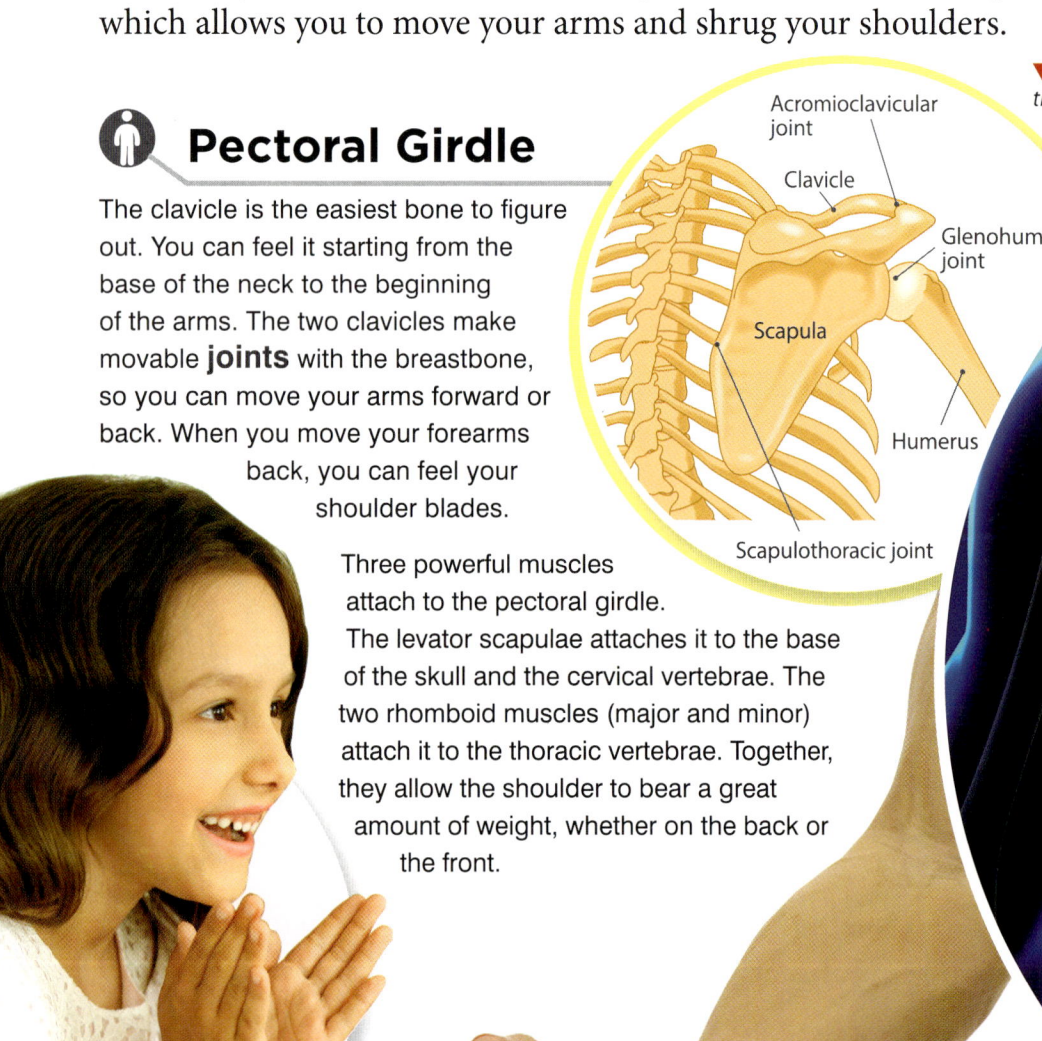

▼ *Close-up view of the pectoral girdle*

- Acromioclavicular joint
- Clavicle
- Glenohumeral joint
- Scapula
- Humerus
- Scapulothoracic joint

▲ *Clapping hands and flapping wings—both actions require the pectoralis major and the pectoral girdle*

HUMAN BODY | SKELETAL & MUSCULAR SYSTEM

 Breastbone

This is a very tough bone in the front of your chest, and it looks like a bony tie. The upper part is the manubrium, to which the clavicles and the first pair of ribs attach. The lower part is the sternum proper, to which the remaining true ribs (2–7) attach. The pectoralis major muscle connects the breastbone, ribs clavicle and scapula to the forearm. Heart surgeons have to break the breastbone to reach the heart during surgery.

Isn't It Amazing!

The breastbone is huge, compared to the body, in birds and bats. This in turn helps the pectoralis major become powerful enough to flap the wings to make them fly.

◄ *The internal skeleton of a bird*

 The Ribs

You have three kinds of ribs. Ribs 1–7 are true ribs as they attach to thoracic vertebrae T1–T7 and to the sternum. Ribs 8–10 are false ribs, named so because they do not attach directly to the sternum, but to rib 7. Ribs 11–12 do not attach to the sternum at all and are called floating ribs.

The head of the rib is the part that attaches to the arch of a thoracic vertebra. A little bump near the head, called the tubercle, attaches to the transverse process. After this, the rib turns sharply toward the chest, forming a C-shape. The ribs do not attach to the sternum directly, but taper into cartilage, which attaches them to the sternum. This allows the rib cage to expand with the lungs when you breathe in air, and contract with the lungs when you breathe out.

◄ *The 7 true ribs attach to the first 7 of the 12 thoracic vertebrae*

▲ *Ribs sticking out of the chest shows that a person is severely underweight*

Inside Your Bones

Our skeleton comprises our bones. But what exactly exists inside each bone? Even though they often feel like nothing but hard, white rods, bones, in fact, have a complex internal structure. Not all bones are the same. Some are much harder than the others, like skull plates. Other bones are spongy and lighter than they feel. Many bones are hollow inside. However, they are filled with a fatty substance called **marrow**. Did you know that this marrow is the place where your blood cells are born?

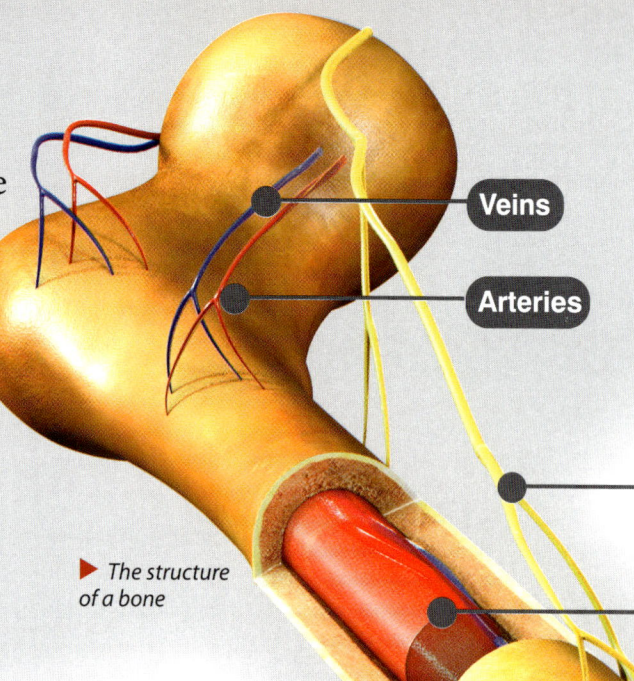

▶ The structure of a bone

The Making of a Bone

We start out as babies with a cartilage skeleton. Each 'bone' has a tissue that covers it, called the periosteum, which gets veins, arteries and lymph vessels. Special cells, called osteogenic cells, migrate to the bone being formed. Some stay as they are until the day that the bones need to be repaired. Most will become **osteoblasts**, which are cells that make **collagen**. Collagen is a protein that forms threads easily, and is seen in **tendons** and **ligaments**, as well as in hair and nails. In the bones, it forms a three-dimensional 'matrix' of woven fibres.

Osteoblasts fill this matrix with calcium hydroxyapatite, a mineral compound made of calcium and phosphorus ($Ca_{10}(PO_4)_6(OH)_2$). The bone matrix may be filled completely with this compound to make compact bone, or leave air gaps to make spongy bone. As the osteoblasts lay down minerals, they get trapped in it and become osteocytes. Osteocytes keep the bone nourished and lay down more mineral if needed.

As we grow, so do our bones. Special cells called **osteoclasts** help in this process. They 'resorb' the minerals so that the bone can become wider and longer, before osteoblasts lay down fresh matrix.

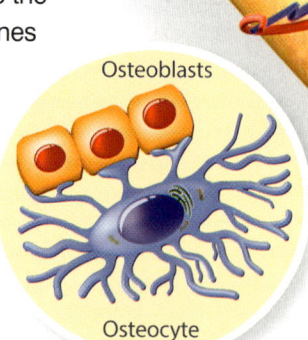

▲ Osteoblasts turn into osteocytes as they deposit bone matrix

◀ Bones do not stay the same throughout life but are constantly remodelled to grow in size and weight as you grow

💡 Isn't It Amazing!

Did you know that shark bones are actually made of cartilage? Cartilage is a light, flexible material made of chondroitin sulphate, hyaluronic acid and collagen fibres. It is also found where bones meet to form a joint.

▶ Sharks are called cartilaginous fish

HUMAN BODY | SKELETAL & MUSCULAR SYSTEM | 11

Incredible Individuals

Scientists believe that the ancestors of our species (*Homo habilis*) first started out as scavengers. They ate meat left behind by other predators. They started making tools out of stone to get to the marrow of left-behind bones, and that was one of the first tools that humankind made.

Bone Marrow

Many bones, like the vertebrae, ribs, sternum, hip bones and bones of the arm and leg are hollow inside and filled with either yellow or red marrow. Yellow marrow is a jelly-like tissue made of fat-storing cells. Red marrow is more complex and is made of stem cells that make the cells of the blood—Red Blood Cells (RBCs), White Blood Cells (WBCs) and platelets.

Until you are seven years old, almost all your marrow is red. After that, most marrow becomes yellow and stops making blood. But if a bad injury or fever with lots of blood loss occurs, yellow marrow can become red again.

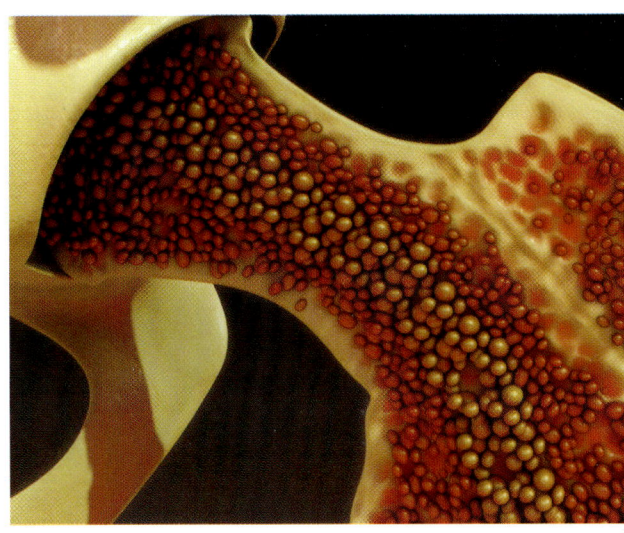

▲ A 3D illustration of bone marrow

Bone Membranes

The inside of a bone is called its medullary cavity. It is lined by a membrane called the endosteum. It contains the bone cells that help the bone grow and also repair it. The outside of a bone is also covered by a membrane called the periosteum. Blood vessels, nerves and lymphatic vessels come to the periosteum, from where nutrients diffuse into the bone. Tendons and ligaments attach at the periosteum. At the joints, the periosteum is replaced by articular cartilage.

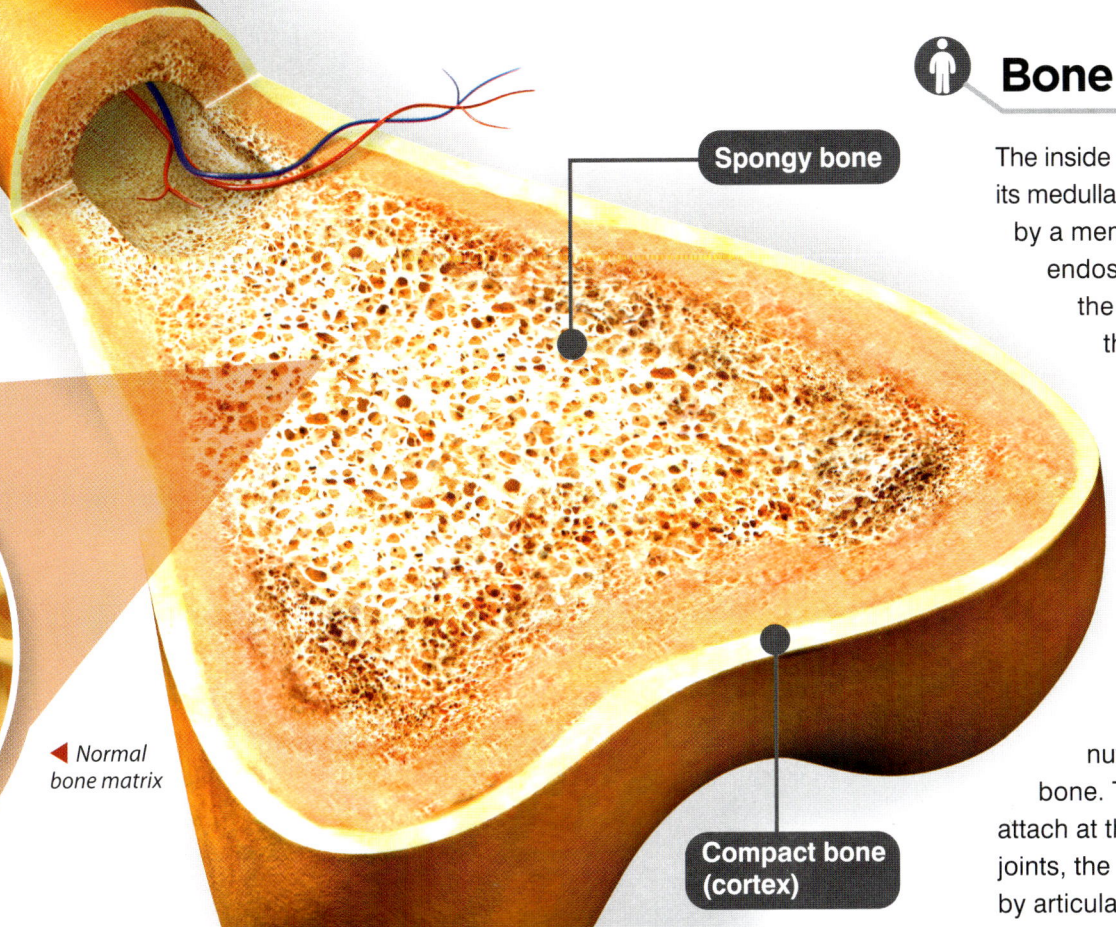

◀ Normal bone matrix

The Bones that Keep Us Going

Every animal needs its arms and legs to move from one place to another. Even when we hear the word 'bone', it is the bones of the arm (**humerus**, **radius** and **ulna**) and the leg (**femur**, **tibia** and **fibula**) that we think of, as they have knobbed endings and long, cylindrical shafts. Why so? Because these are the bones we frequently see on the dinner plate. Let us see how they fit into the limbs, and how they work.

Upper Arm and Forearm

Your arm is made of three parts—the upper arm, the forearm and the hand. The upper arm extends from your shoulder to your elbow. It has only one bone—the humerus bone—in it. It is attached to some very powerful muscles like the latissimus dorsi in the back and the pectoralis major in the chest, which help raise or lower your arms, and move them forward or back. It also has two major muscles that run alongside it, the **biceps brachii** and the **triceps**. The biceps pull the forearm towards you, while the triceps extend it again.

The head of the humerus bone meets the shoulder blade to form the glenohumeral joint. At the other end, it has the trochlea, a pulley-shaped area that joints with the ulna, and the capitulum (little head) that joints with the radius. Together, these make the elbow.

The forearm has two bones, the shorter radius and the longer ulna. They join at the elbow to make the proximal radioulnar joint, and at the wrist to make the distal radioulnar joint. These let you rotate the forearm. The triceps attaches to the ulna, while the biceps attaches to the radius.

◀ People lift weights to exercise and strengthen their muscles

◀ The humerus is called the funny bone because it has the same pronunciation as the word 'humorous'

Isn't It Amazing!

The flight muscles in vultures are some of the strongest in the world, taking them as high as 37,000 feet above sea level.

HUMAN BODY — SKELETAL & MUSCULAR SYSTEM

◀ Our nervous system helps the bones and muscles of the arms and legs coordinate with each other, and also with the spine, for smooth body movements

In Real Life

The femur bears the weight of the body when we stand. It can bear a load of up to 1100 kilograms.

▶ The position of the femur and tibia while the body is in action

Thigh and Foreleg

Like your arm, your leg too is made of three parts—the thigh, the foreleg and the foot. The thigh extends from your hip to your knee and has only one bone in it—the femur. It is attached to some of the most powerful muscles in your body. These are the **gluteus** muscles in the back and the adductor muscles in the front, which raise or lower your thighs, and move them forward or backward for walking. It also has two major muscles that run alongside it, the biceps femoris and the quadriceps. The biceps pulls the foreleg towards you, while the quadriceps extends it again.

The head of the femur meets the hip to form the hip joint. At the other end, it has the epicondyles, a pulley-shaped area that joins with the tibia to make the knee. It does not meet the fibula. A small bone called the patella caps the knee.

The foreleg has two bones, the shorter, fibula, and the longer, tibia. They join below the knee to make the proximal tibiofibular joint, and at the ankle to make the distal tibiofibular joint. These let you rotate the leg. The calf muscles run alongside them, from the femur to the anklebone.

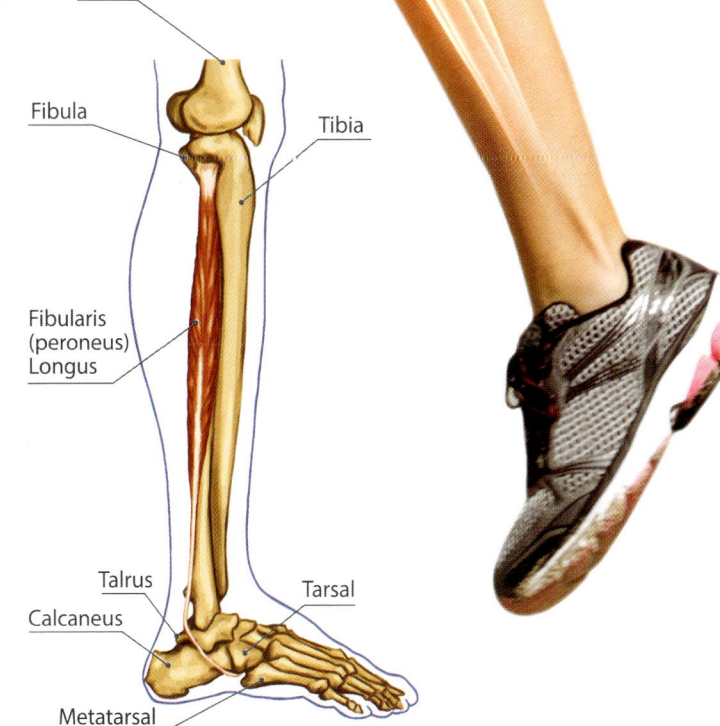

▲ The femur and tibia are the longest and second-longest bones of your body

In Your Hands and Feet

The bones of the hands and feet are similar in structure, because we evolved from animals that used them both for walking. But as they evolved to do utterly different things, small changes happened over millions of years to make them look quite unlike each other. The biggest difference was the change in the way the thumb works. It can 'oppose' the other fingers, which helps you pick up things, hold chopsticks, write letters or catch a basketball. The big toe on the foot cannot do all this, but it helps you balance while you stand on tiptoe, as your hands reach out for a jar from the top shelf.

Isn't It Amazing!

Chimps have thumbs too, but these are not as flexible as ours. We owe it to the flexor pollicis longus, the muscle in our thumbs that makes it possible to pinch and grip the tiniest of things.

▶ Chimps also have opposable big toes that help them climb trees

The Hand

While the arm has only 3 bones, the hand has 27. All these bones give the hand the flexibility it needs to do the hundreds of things that you do in a day. You can handle a mobile phone, type on a computer keyboard, use a spoon and fork, climb into the school bus, hold your books or even bite your nails.

Each finger has three **phalanges**, while the thumb only has two. They are jointed so you can make a grip, but you cannot bend them outwards. If you feel the back of your hand, you can make out the five **metacarpals**, which have the little muscles that help you move your fingers. The wrist is made of eight **carpals**. These little bones give the wrist an amazing level of flexibility as they make many joints and attach many little muscles, so you can rotate your hand, move it sideways or up and down.

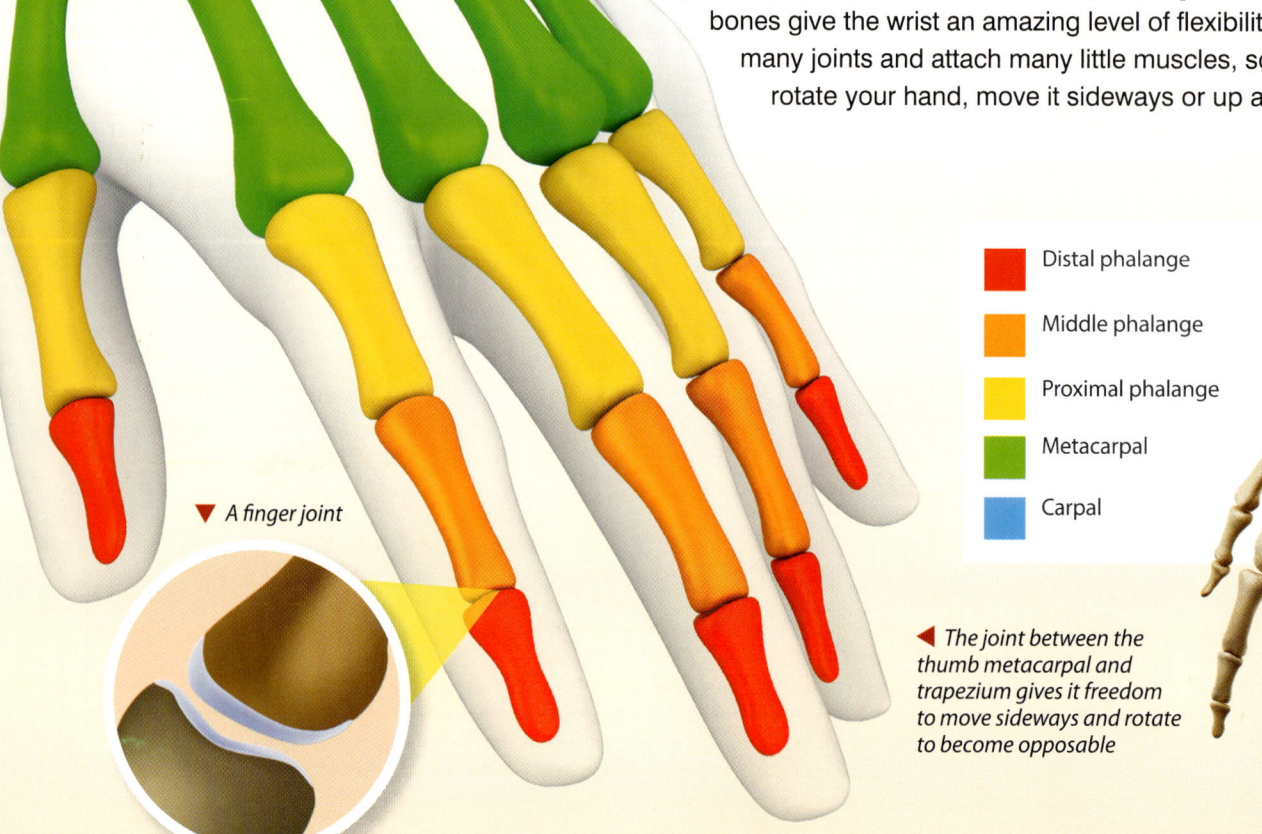

▼ A finger joint

- Distal phalange
- Middle phalange
- Proximal phalange
- Metacarpal
- Carpal

◀ The joint between the thumb metacarpal and trapezium gives it freedom to move sideways and rotate to become opposable

The Foot

Like the hand, the foot too has 26 bones. Unlike the hands though, these bones do not give the feet flexibility. But they help them bear the enormous load of your body, whether you are standing, walking or running.

Each toe has three phalanges, but only the first and part of the second are free. The rest are locked inside the foot. Like the metacarpals of the hand, the **metatarsals** make up the sole of the foot. They are long and make up the 'flat feet' that help you balance while standing. The seven **tarsals** help transfer the weight of the body to the ground, and also help with rotating your feet, and moving them up, down or sideways. The largest tarsals are the talus, which make your ankle bone, and the calcaneus, which make your heel. The calcaneus, tarsals and metatarsals make up the longitudinal arch of the foot. The arch absorbs energy when the foot is pressed down when walking and releases it when the foot is raised—giving you the 'spring' in your step.

▲ The illustration shows the bones of the flat foot

▶ The bones of the feet have powerful ligaments attached to them, which act as shock absorbers

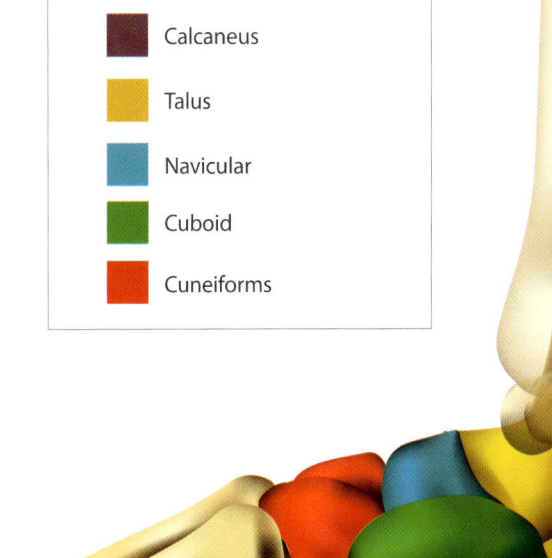

- Calcaneus
- Talus
- Navicular
- Cuboid
- Cuneiforms

Becoming Bipedal

Bipedal refers to animals that walk on two feet. Among the apes, we are the only ones to have become exclusively bipedal. For this, the bones of the legs had to be modified in three ways. First, the femur, fibula and tibia modified to form a pillar upon which the body's weight is balanced while standing. Second, the bones of the heel modified to act as a counterbalance to those of the feet. As we walk, the body transfers its weight from one leg to the other through the thighs and heels. Third, the joints modified to allow the legs to stride without buckling while walking.

Incredible Individuals

Achilles was a mythical Greek hero who could not be hurt anywhere except in his heel. The phrase "Achilles' heel" now means an unsuspected weakness.

▶ According to the myth, Achilles' mum dipped him in the Styx, when he was a baby, to make him immortal, but since she held him by the heel, that part remained mortal

Some Very Hip Bones

Today, most people lead a sedentary lifestyle. You might find yourself sitting a lot while writing surprise tests at school, playing mobile games in the bus, having dinner, watching TV or doing homework. Our hip takes all the stress of this sitting. Originally meant to support the spine and the hindlegs, your hip bones evolved to attach powerful muscles. In women, they also need to bear the weight of a whole baby as it grows within them. Then the baby comes out through the birth canal, parting the hip bones.

▼ *The gluteus muscles attached to the hip give it both strength and flexibility*

Structure

When you are growing up, your hip is made of three pairs of bones—the large ilium, the ischium and the pubis. By the time you are 18 years old, they will have fused to form just two hip bones that together make the **pelvic girdle**. The ilium is the largest, uppermost part. You can feel its top (iliac crest) just below your waist. These fleshy muscles also make up your bottom and cushion you while you sit. The insides of the ilium are cup-shaped and hold the inner organs in them.

The ischium and pubis make arches that merge at the bottom of your torso. Between them, they contain the obturator foramen, which lets the blood vessels and nerves of the legs pass through, and also the muscles that connect to the thigh. The outside of the ilium, ischium and pubis make a cup-like shape called the acetabulum, where the femur makes a joint.

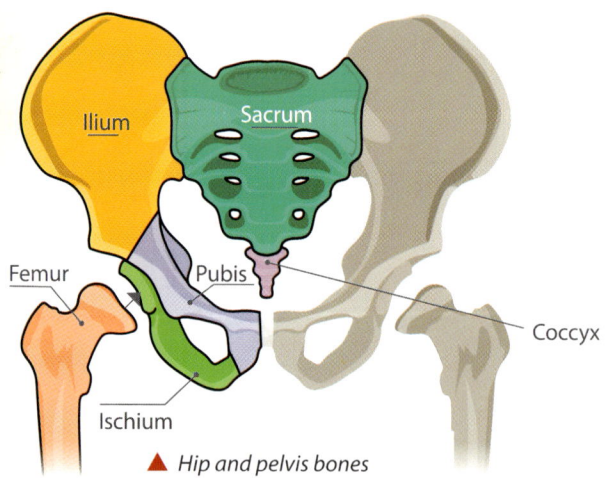

▲ *Hip and pelvis bones*

Pelvis

The hip bones and the lower spine (sacrum and coccyx) together make up the pelvis. They are linked by a number of ligaments that allow you a lot of freedom to twist your lower body, compared to the legs. Without the pelvis, you wouldn't be able to dance. It also allows your bottom to spread out when you are sitting, so that you do not feel cramped up.

Helping You Move
Skeletal Joints

Your skeleton would make you as stiff as a statue if there weren't any joints in it. The joints give the bones the space they need to move. They work on the principle of levers, and act as the fulcrum in which the load (bone) is moved by the effort (muscle). Joints can be classified according to the amount of mobility they provide (functional classification), or the kind of material that links the bones (structural classification). Some joints are temporary. They vanish as you grow up and the bones fuse together.

Functional Classification

You can classify joints into three types this way:

- Synarthroses, which do not allow the bones to move at all, like the sutures of the skull.
- Amphiarthroses allow some movement, like the intervertebral discs and the symphysis pubis between the hip bones.
- Diarthroses allow a lot of movement between the bones. Diarthroses are further classified into:
  - Uniaxial joints, which allow up and down movements only (fingers, elbows, knees).
  - Biaxial joints, which allow up and down, and sideways movements (wrists and ankles).
  - Multiaxial joints, which allow up and down, sideways and rotational movements (hips and shoulders).

In Real Life

Joints and muscles work as type II levers, the joint as fulcrum and the muscle as effort, with the bone serving as load.

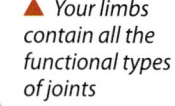
▲ Your limbs contain all the functional types of joints

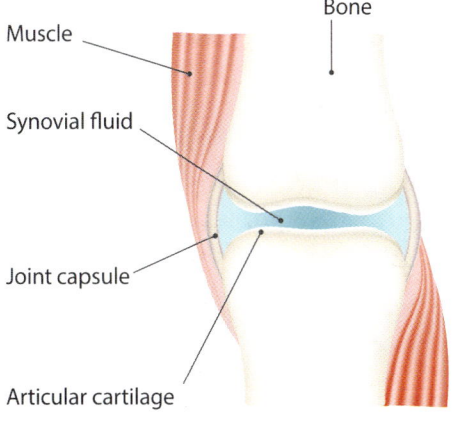
▲ The structure of a joint

Structural Classification

Joints are classified as fibrous, cartilaginous and synovial, depending on how they are made. Fibrous joints are connected by collagen fibres, such as those between teeth and jaws. In cartilaginous joints, cartilage fills the spaces between bones like the **cranial sutures**. Synovial joints are complex, with **synovial fluid** lubricating the joints.

How Joints Work

A skeleton may appear creepy, but observing it will help you understand how our bodies move. The joints you see here are all synovial diarthroses, meaning they allow plenty of movement and are lubricated by synovial fluid.

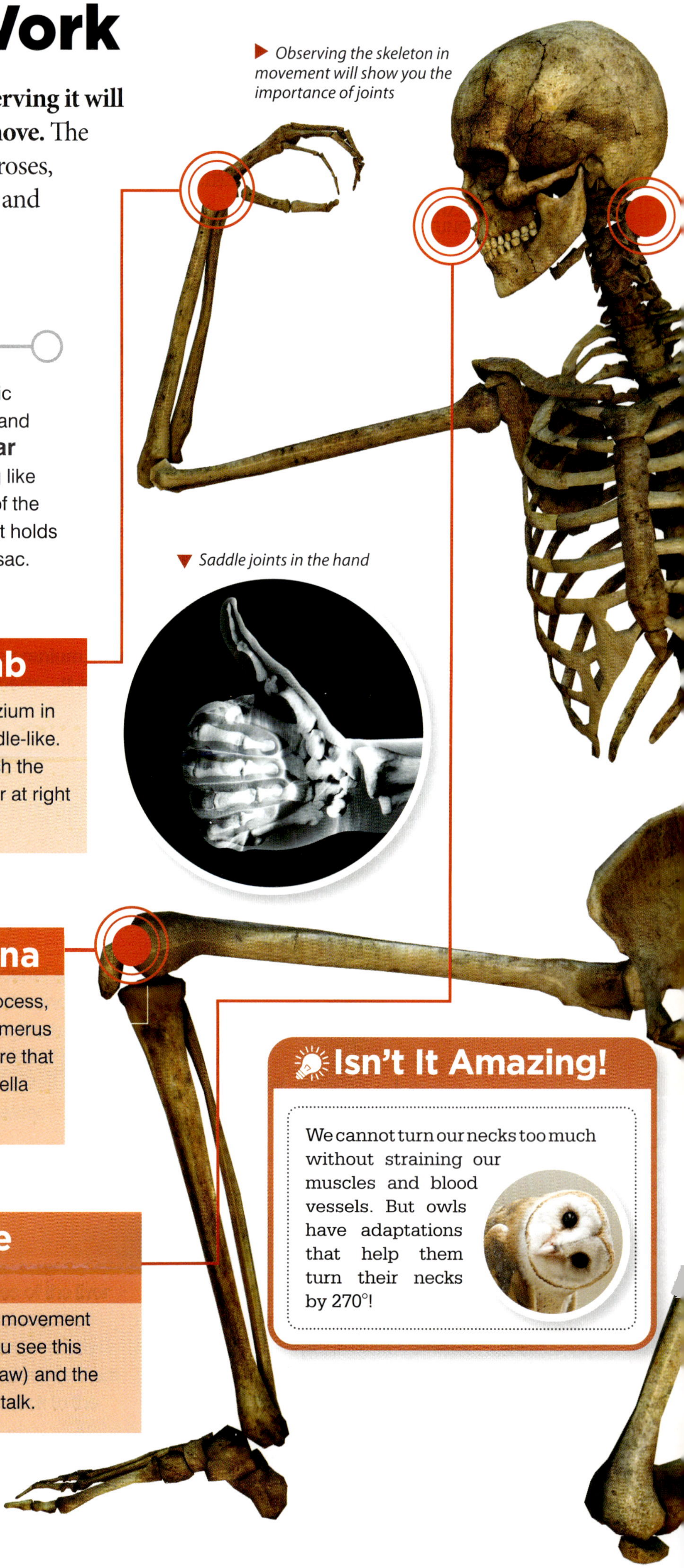

▶ Observing the skeleton in movement will show you the importance of joints

More about Joints

Synovial fluid is made of plasma from the blood that is rich in nutrients. It also contains hyaluronic acid, which acts a bit like engine oil. It is elastic and viscous, preventing friction in the joint. **Articular cartilage** covers the ends of the bones, acting like a shock absorber. The rest of the joint is made of the periosteum of both the bones, making a sac that holds the synovial fluid in. So, it is called the synovial sac.

▼ Saddle joints in the hand

Saddle: Wrist & thumb

The metacarpal of the thumb meets the trapezium in this joint. Both the faces of the bones are saddle-like. Hold your thumb and forefinger apart to stretch the web between them. Bring both hands together at right angles and you can see how this joint works.

Hinge: Humerus & Ulna

The upper end of the ulna is the olecranon process, which locks into the olecranon fossa of the humerus when the arm is stretched fully. This makes sure that the forearm does not bend backward. The patella does the same job in the knee.

Isn't It Amazing!

We cannot turn our necks too much without straining our muscles and blood vessels. But owls have adaptations that help them turn their necks by 270°!

Bicondylar: Mandible & Temporal Bones

This joint allows both hinge-like and sideways movement to the extent that the skin can be stretched. You see this best in the joint between the mandible (lower jaw) and the temporal bone, which lets you chew food and talk.

HUMAN BODY | SKELETAL & MUSCULAR SYSTEM

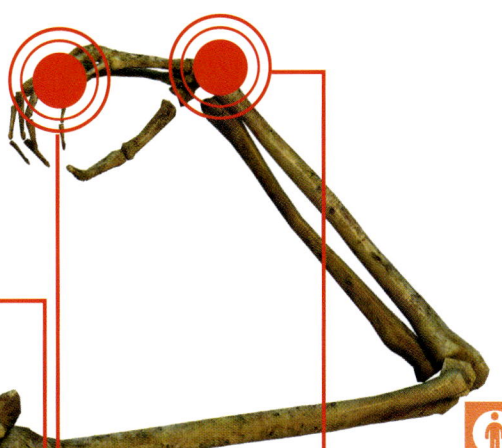

⭐ Incredible Individuals

Tommy John's baseball career was finished in 1974 when his elbow ligament was torn. A new surgical procedure got him back in play. He went on to win 164 matches. It is now called the Tommy John Surgery in the USA.

Gliding: Wrist bones

The eight carpals of the wrist have flat faces facing each other. This allows them to glide over each other a bit. Nevertheless, the wrist helps your hand move in all three planes (sideways, up-down and rotational). The tarsals also work this way.

Condyloid & Ellipsoid: Carpal and Forefinger

This joint allows a little movement up and down and a little sideways. You see this in the joint between your palm and your forefinger. It allows all movement except axial rotation. An example of the condyloid joint is the ovoid head of one bone moving into the elliptical cavity of another. This joint is seen in the wrist and the base of the index finger.

Pivot: Axis & Atlas

The dens of the axis (second cervical vertebra) is the pivot onto which the hollow body of the atlas (first vertebra) fits, making a perfect pivot that lets you turn your neck about 100° on each side.

Ball & Socket: Femur and Hip

The head of the femur is shaped like a ball, which fits into the acetabulum of the hip. Several ligaments and muscles help the joint move in three ways—forward and backward (walking), raising and lowering the leg sideways, and rotating the leg horizontally. The humerus and shoulder joint works the same way.

Ligaments

Ligaments connect two bones to each other at the joints. They are made of tough sheets of collagen, so that they don't tear when the muscles stretch out those bones. Proximal ligaments are close to the synovial sac, while remote ligaments attach to their bones further away.

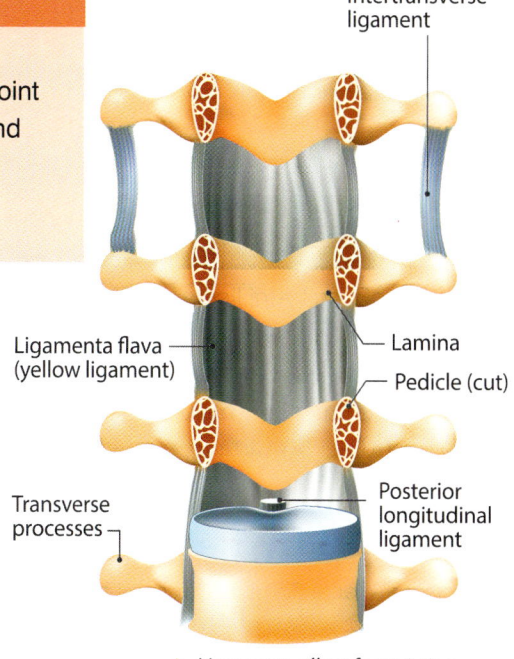

▲ *Ligaments allow for twisting movements of the spine.*

Breaking Point
Bone Fractures

Although our bones are strong enough to take the stresses and strains of daily life, they are also brittle. This means that though they are hard, under great force, they can break or shatter. Depending on how you get hurt, fractures can happen in different ways. Fractures often occur in childhood, when the bones have not become hard enough. **Osteoporosis** and bone cancer leave them likely to break in an accident. Excessive force and trauma suffered during accidents can also lead to fractures.

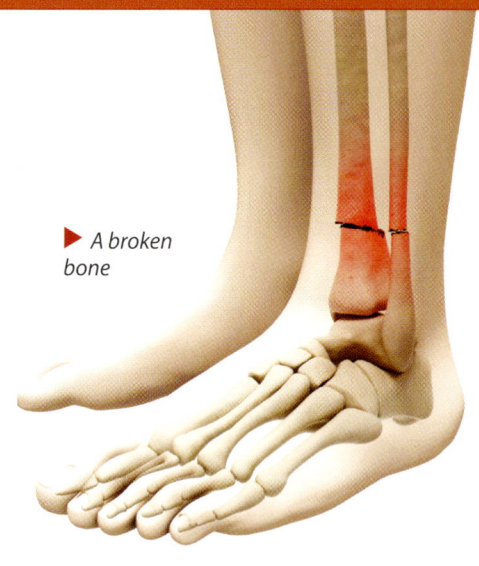
▶ A broken bone

Types of Fractures

Doctors must consider how a fracture happens before they can set it right and put it in plaster. A closed or simple fracture stays within the skin; but if you get hurt so badly that the bone breaks and tears out of the skin, it is an open or compound fracture. These are harder to set right as they may pierce organs and may require complicated surgery. Doctors also classify fractures in different ways.

Isn't It Amazing!

Boa constrictors do not have enough force to crush bones, as was thought earlier. But they can definitely suffocate their prey.

▶ Boas kill their prey by squeezing them hard enough to stop their hearts

▼ Transverse fracture  It happens across the width of the bone

▼ Longitudinal fracture 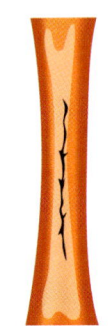 It happens along the length of a bone

▼ Oblique bone fracture  It happens at an angle

▼ Spiral fracture 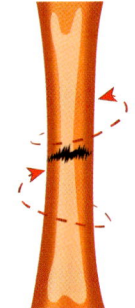 It happens when the broken parts of the bone get twisted

▼ Greenstick fracture  It happens when only one side is broken

▼ Comminuted fracture  It refers to many breaks in the bone leading to splinters

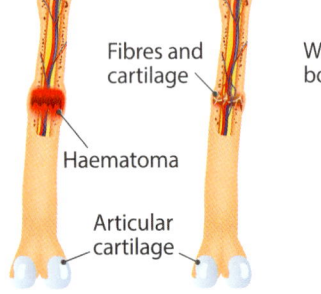 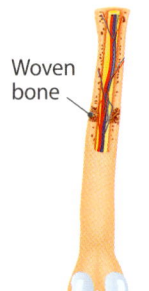 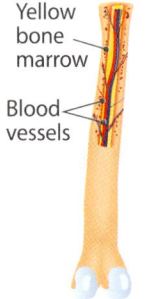

Haematoma formation | Fibrocartilaginous callus formation | Bony callus formation | Bone remodelling

▲ Bone repair is carried out by osteogenic cells, which multiply to make new osteoblast cells

Bone Healing

Bones heal very quickly after fracturing. The blood vessels that get broken in the fracture make a thick clot between the bones, called a haematoma. Osteogenic cells from the periosteum secrete fibres and cartilage to 'stitch' the bones together, forming a callus. In the next few weeks, new bone cells grow inside the callus, the blood vessels reconnect, and the bone marrow also regrows.

Moving Our Bodies
Muscles and Tendons

Say muscle and you immediately think of the bulging biceps and triceps of weightlifters, or the powerful muscles in the legs of athletes. But did you know that the organ with the most muscles is your face? It has hundreds of tiny muscles that allow you to make lots of expressions, and convey emotions, from smiling to frowning, and from demoting anger to fright and even laughter.

In Real Life

The muscles of the eye are at work all the time you are awake, repositioning the eye every time you move your head. In an hour, they may contract and relax over 10,000 times.

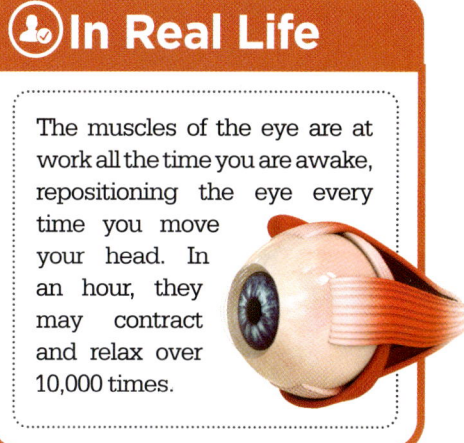

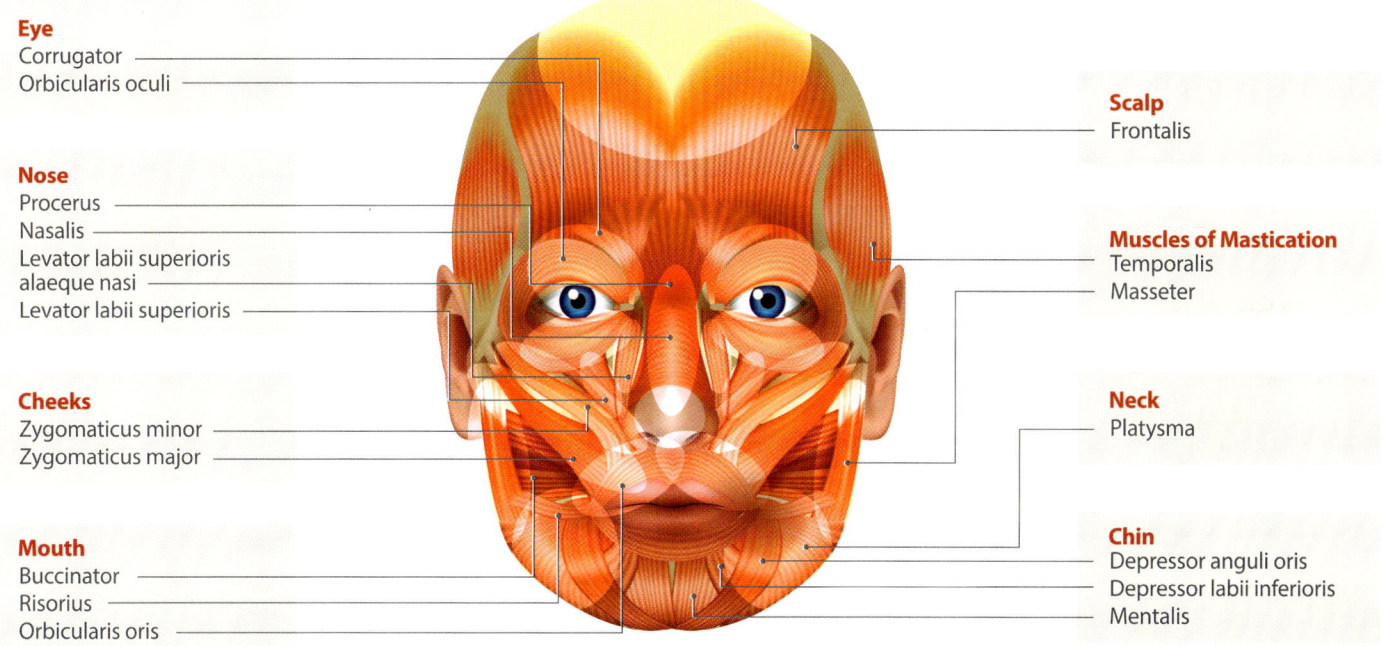

Eye
Corrugator
Orbicularis oculi

Nose
Procerus
Nasalis
Levator labii superioris alaeque nasi
Levator labii superioris

Cheeks
Zygomaticus minor
Zygomaticus major

Mouth
Buccinator
Risorius
Orbicularis oris

Scalp
Frontalis

Muscles of Mastication
Temporalis
Masseter

Neck
Platysma

Chin
Depressor anguli oris
Depressor labii inferioris
Mentalis

▲ The diagram shows some of the muscles of your face

Muscles in the Head

There are other muscles too, which do their work without you ever finding out. They help you with breathing and digesting food, with keeping blood flowing through your veins and arteries, and urine flowing out of your body. A very special kind of muscle keeps your heart pumping throughout life. Let us find out what muscles are, and how they work.

Types of Muscles

After many years of study, doctors and scientists say that muscles come in three types:

- **Striated muscles** are fibre-like in shape and are attached to your bones. You move them as you wish.
- **Smooth muscles** are circular in shape. They are attached to your internal organs, and move on their own.
- **Cardiac muscles** are halfway between striated and smooth muscles. They are present in the heart and also move on their own.

Tendons

Striated muscles hold onto their bones with tissues called tendons. A tendon is like a piece of elastic, able to stretch and hold a lot of strain as the muscles contract and expand. They are made of collagen. On one side, the tendon merges with the muscle, and on the other, it merges with the coating of the bones (periosteum).

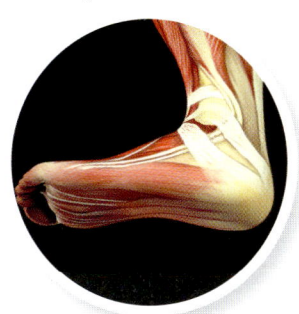

▲ Tendons (white) reduce strain on your muscles (red)

The Muscles We Can Control

▶ *Regular exercise keeps your muscles healthy*

Much of your body's weight is made of muscle. Most of it is made of skeletal muscles. Whether you reach out an arm to catch a ball, pull your stomach in to exhale, smile at someone or run away from a cockroach, your skeletal muscles are doing the majority of the work. That is why they are called voluntary muscles. They act when you want them to.

Muscle Tissue

Under a microscope, muscle tissue looks like long streaks of threads. The scientists' name for this is striation, these are therefore called striated muscles too. Most of the meat you eat is made of the same kind of muscle.

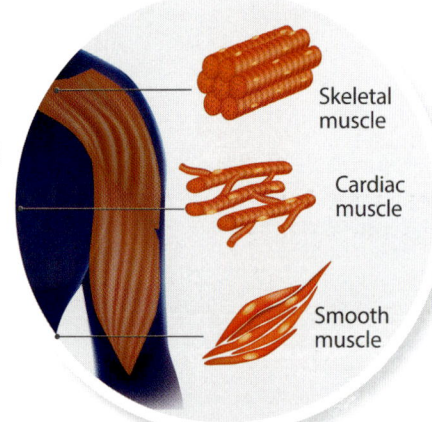

▲ *Types of muscles*

Under the Microscope

The part of the muscle that does all the work is the **myofibril**. It is made up of proteins called actin and myosin. These myofibrils are inside muscle cells called sarcomeres and are attached to the covering membrane of the cell, called the sarcolemma. Each muscle cell has hundreds of mitochondria to give it instant energy. It is also connected to the nervous system by **neuromuscular junctions**, which allow you to control the muscle.

The sarcomeres are bound together in bundles called fascicles. Lots of fascicles together make a muscle, along with blood vessels and connective tissue. Connective tissue is made of cells that help feed cells to the muscles and also make the muscle flexible. It is made of three layers—the endomysium surrounding the fascicles, the perimysium connecting them, and the epimysium wrapping around the muscle.

💡 Isn't It Amazing!

Cheetahs do not have stronger muscles than any other big cats, but the muscles of their forelimbs pack in more sarcomeres, end-to-end, in each fascicle. This helps them attain speeds of up to 29 mps when chasing prey, and that is what makes them the fastest animal on Earth.

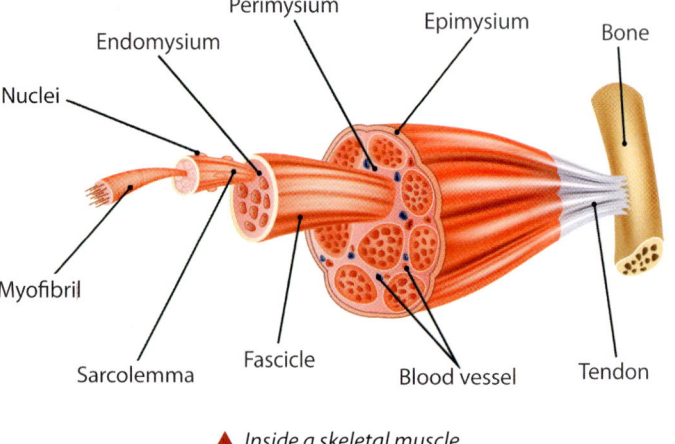

▲ *Inside a skeletal muscle*

The Muscles We Cannot Control

The big muscles that attach to our bones and make up most of our body are important. However, alongside them are thousands of tinier muscles that work throughout our lives without resting. They are the involuntary muscles. They are connected to our sympathetic and parasympathetic muscles, so we generally do not have control over them (although some, like the muscles of our eyelids, are both voluntary and involuntary). They do not have stripes when you see them under a microscope, so they are also called smooth muscles.

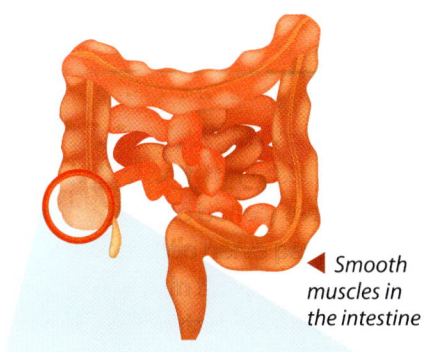

◀ Smooth muscles in the intestine

 ## Finding Smooth Muscles

Many of these muscles are present in the walls of our intestines, making food go along; our arteries and veins, making blood go along; and in the urinary bladder, making sure urine does not leak until we are ready. Some control valves in the blood vessels. Other muscles, like sphincters, act like valves themselves in the digestive system. As these are ring-shaped, they are called circular muscles. Other smooth muscles help the lungs contract and expand. Muscles in the uterus allow women to give birth.

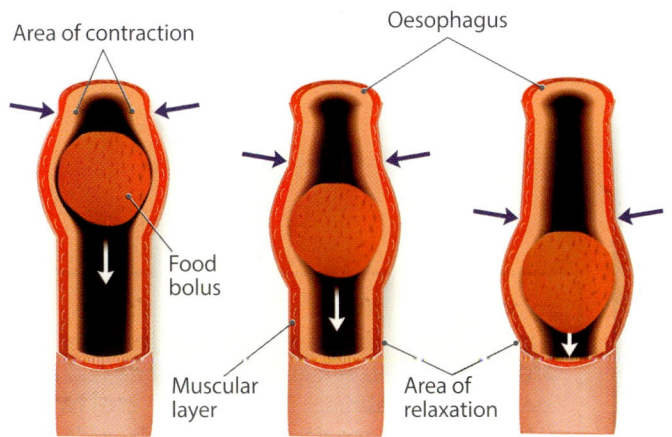

▲ Rings of smooth muscle in the food pipe contract and expand to push food along. This is called peristalsis

In Real Life

Most muscles are relaxed when not at work. Sphincters are different. They are usually closed, so that things do not leak from one organ to another, like from the stomach to the food pipe, or from the small intestine to the stomach.

▲ When sphincters cannot close, they cause upsets like acid refluxes

 ## A Closer Look

Smooth muscles look a bit like stretched rugby balls or insect cocoons. They are not organised into fascicles like skeletal muscles, but are surrounded by endomysium. Dense bodies help tether the myofibrils to the sarcolemma and intermediate filaments connect all the dense bodies. This helps pull all the thick filaments (myosin) and thin filaments (actin) together when the muscle contracts. Motor neurones of the autonomic nervous system make junctions with all the muscle cells to help them coordinate their contraction and relaxation.

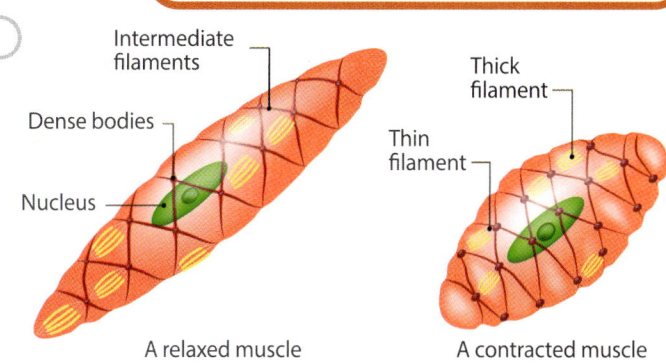

▲ Smooth muscles do not need as much energy as skeletal muscles, but they do not need to produce as much force either

How Muscles Work

Bodybuilders and weightlifters love showing off the bulge in their biceps as they contract. They have exercised a lot for those big muscles, but what are they made of? Why do they appear so strong? How come the muscle bulge is not there when their hands are stretched out or relaxed?

◀ A bodybuilder contracts the muscles of his arm

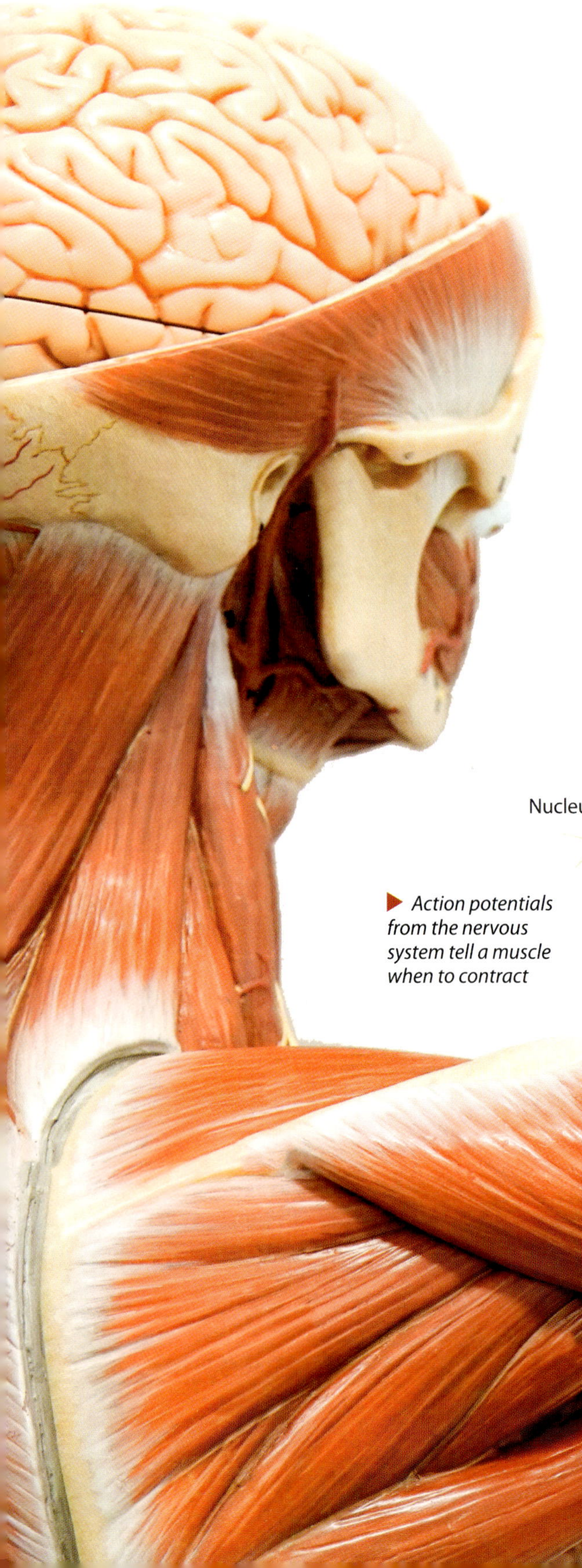

Why Muscles Bulge

Muscles cells contain proteins that do all the hard work. The two main ones are actin and myosin, which form thread-like filaments. Myosin has 'heads', which can stick to actin. When the muscle is at rest, the actin and myosin filaments are apart, and the muscle is flat. When the muscle contracts, millions of actin-myosin pairs are pulled together and the muscle bulges out from the body.

Neuromuscular Junctions

Your muscles are connected to motor neurones through tiny synapses called Neuromuscular Junctions (NMJ). When your muscles have to contract, they get a signal from the brain or spinal cord in the form of a tiny electric current. This current reaches the NMJ, and a chemical called a neurotransmitter is released. It creates a new current across the muscle fibres.

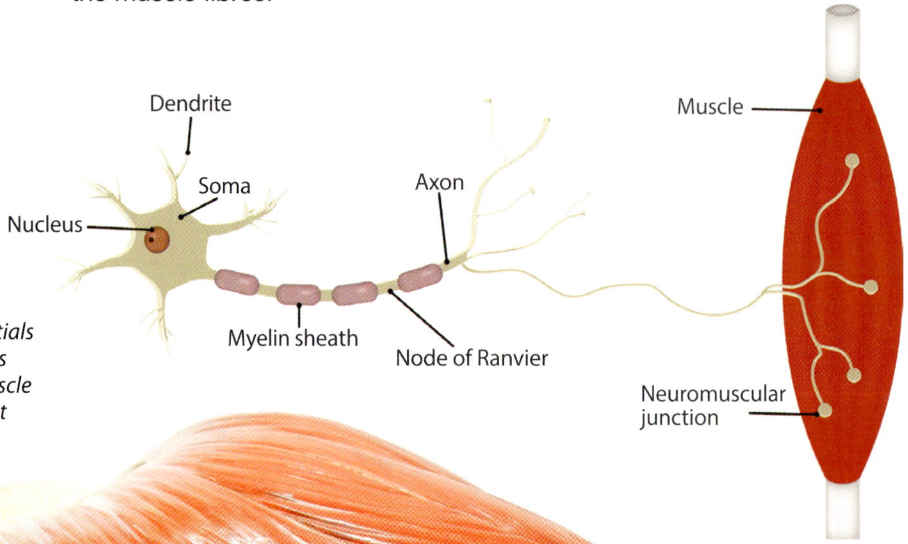

▶ Action potentials from the nervous system tell a muscle when to contract

HUMAN BODY — SKELETAL & MUSCULAR SYSTEM

Action Potential

This is a tiny electric current that passes along the length of a muscle fibre. When there is no message from the brain, there is sodium (Na+) outside the neurone and potassium (K+) and chloride (Cl–) inside the muscle cells. This is the resting potential. When a signal arrives, Na+ rushes in and K+ rushes out, creating the action potential. As the muscle relaxes, the two slowly switch places again.

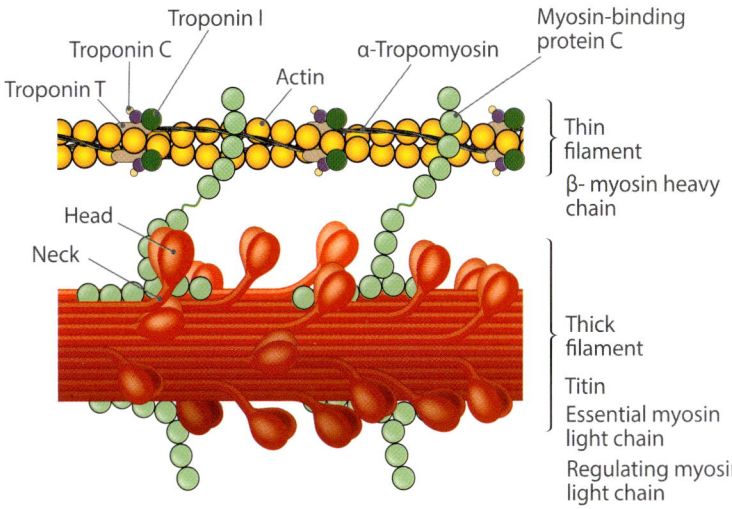

▶ Lots of different proteins work together to make a muscle contract and relax

A Muscle in Action

When the brain sends a signal to the muscle to work, it contracts. Like two magnets that stick to each other, the myosin heads and actin filaments stick to each other. The filaments are pulled closer. The sarcomeres become shorter but thicker. As this happens all over the muscle, it bulges out of the body.

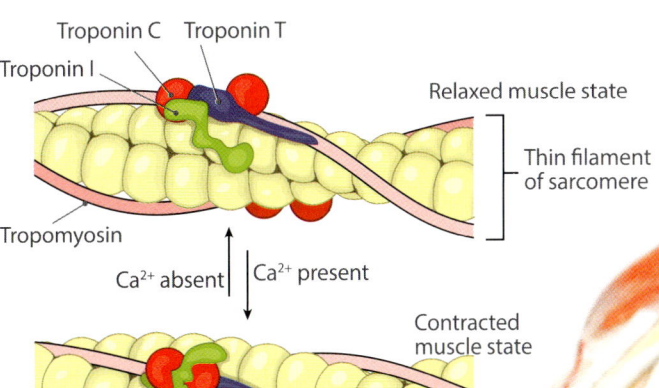

▲ Muscles contract and relax due to the action of calcium ions on the troponin complex

Isn't It Amazing!

Muscles work faster at high temperatures and slower at low temperatures. Warm-blooded animals like birds and mammals maintain a constant body temperature, whatever the weather is, so that their muscles can react quickly to signals from the brain. This helps them run or fly away quickly if faced with danger. Cold-blooded animals like insects and reptiles depend upon the weather being warm to be active.

Relaxing the Muscle

To relax the muscle again, the body needs to carry out respiration. Enzymes in the muscle cells convert glucose into carbon dioxide and water. This gives out a lot of energy. Some of it is trapped in a molecule called ATP, while the rest goes out as body heat. ATP attaches to the heads of the myosin filaments, causing them to detach from the actin filaments. The filaments come apart, the sarcomeres flatten and the muscle thus relaxes.

▲ Yoga can relieve muscular tension

Keeping the Heart Going

After the brain, the heart is our body's most important organ, pumping blood throughout life without a rest. Most of the heart tissue is made of a thick, muscular layer that doctors call the **myocardium**. The muscle cells in it (cardiac muscles) are like voluntary muscles in some ways, and like involuntary muscles in other ways. This makes it possible for them to expand and contract without ever getting tired. Cardiac muscles are controlled by special cells called pacemaker cells, which are connected to the parasympathetic nervous system, and which make sure that you get a regular heartbeat. They get blood from the coronary artery.

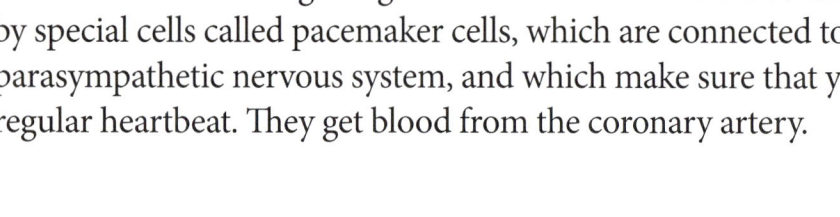

Cardiac Muscle

Cardiac muscles are made of sarcomeres, just like skeletal muscles, but these are shorter and more branched. The branches connect them to each other, through intercalated discs. These allow the cells to pass action potentials between them and also contain desmosomes, which act like clips that hold the muscles together. This makes it possible for the muscles to contract and expand together. The muscles are organised in layers around the heart, so that it pumps smoothly every time it gets a signal from the pacemaker.

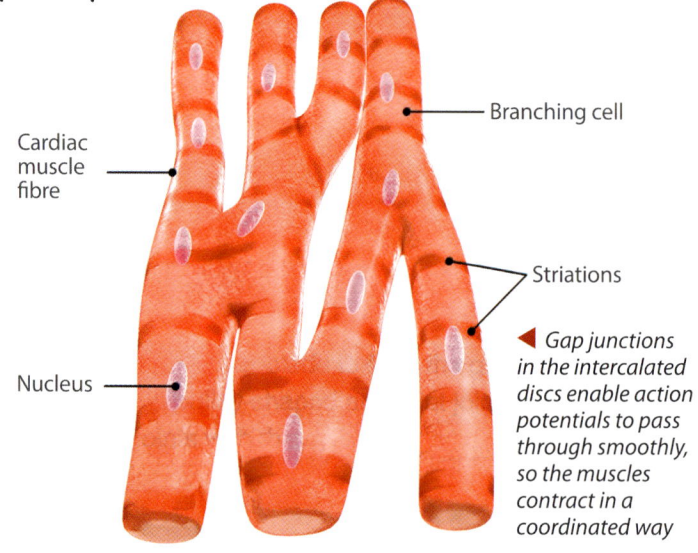

◀ *Gap junctions in the intercalated discs enable action potentials to pass through smoothly, so the muscles contract in a coordinated way*

Pacemakers

The vagus nerve connects the heart to the parasympathetic nervous system. It forms neuromuscular junctions with the pacemaker cells. The nervous system gives regular electric pulses to these cells in the form of action potentials, which travel throughout the heart through the gap junctions.

Artificial pacemakers work in a way similar to the vagus nerve. They are placed in the chests of people with heart arrhythmia, so they can get a tiny electrical current that makes the heart beat with normal rhythm.

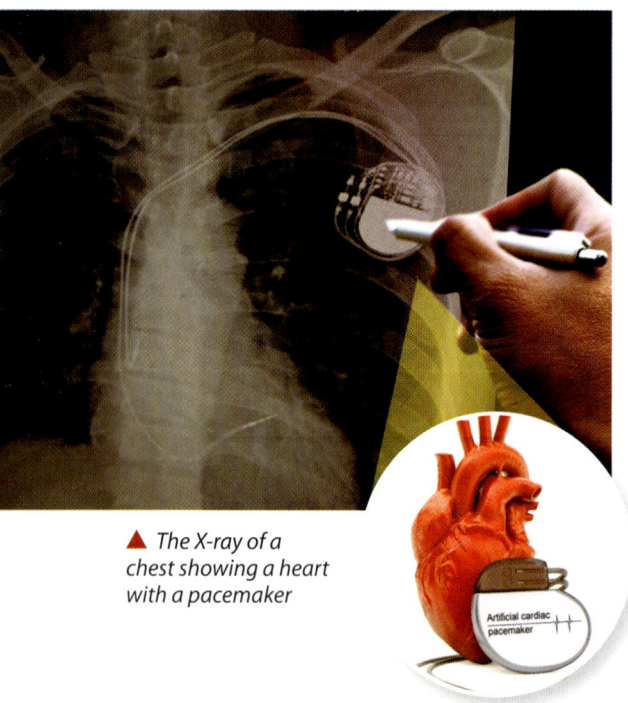

▲ *The X-ray of a chest showing a heart with a pacemaker*

Incredible Individuals

Willem Einthoven got the Nobel Prize in 1924 for inventing the electrocardiogram, which can measure electric currents in the myocardium.

Exercise in Moderation

Regular exercise or play keeps your bones and muscles healthy. Your muscles maintain their strength and flexibility, your circulation improves and oxygen reaches all tissues. Exercise helps you put on more muscle mass, as the protein you eat is turned into new muscle cells and muscle fibres.

Exercise Rules

It is important to warm up before you begin to exercise. Your muscles spend little energy while at rest, but when you start exercising, playing or working, they need to quickly speed up, so they can burn a lot more sugar and get energy. A brisk walk makes them spend thrice as much energy and heavy exercise makes them spend up to 12 times of energy. After exercise, you must do some cool-down exercises to bring your body back to its resting state.

▲ *Team exercises not only improve physical health, but also allow you to make friends and improve coordination*

▼ *Playing or exercising without warming up could give you a cramp*

Cramps

Too much strain on your muscles, or sudden stretching can give you muscle cramps. This happens when the muscle contracts but cannot expand. It is painful and stops you from using the muscle. Swimming in cold water can give you swimmer's cramp, which can be dangerous as it may cause drowning.

Why We Get Tired

When the muscles are at work, they need a lot of energy quickly. Instead of waiting for oxygen, they switch to **anaerobic respiration**. Glucose is broken down into lactic acid and the energy released is used for contracting and expanding the muscles. The increase in lactic acid causes biochemical changes in the muscle tissue, and it begins to slow down after some time. This leads to tiredness. It makes the body rest, and in that time, the lactic acid is broken down to carbon dioxide by **aerobic respiration**. The muscles come back to normal.

▶ *Rotating between different yoga poses is a good way to warm up and cool down*

Getting Older

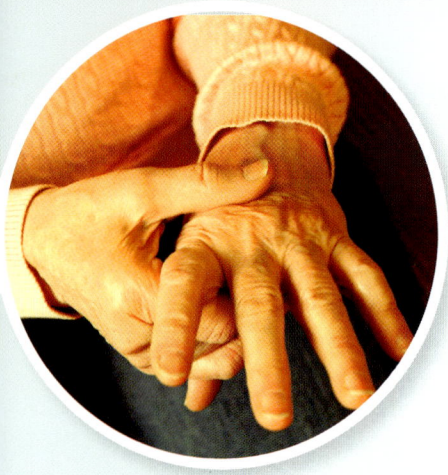

Arthritis means inflammation of the joints, while rheumatism is a condition that affects tendons and ligaments. Spondylitis is an inflammation of the vertebral column. The inflammation affects the cartilage that surrounds the joints and sometimes also the nerves of the muscles that move these joints. These diseases cause severe disabilities because they make it painful to move the joints. It gets difficult to lift weights and walk. These diseases usually affect older people, as their joints wear away due to tissue degeneration. But younger people may get them due to infection, obesity and nutritional deficiencies.

Osteoarthritis

Osteoarthritis or degenerative joint disease is very common. Patients suffer from a lot of pain in their joints of the knees, hip and fingers, because the cartilage that cushions the joints has worn away. The pain sets in after they have been active for a few hours and lasts for a long time. Sometimes, there is a crackling sound (crepitus) as the patient moves.

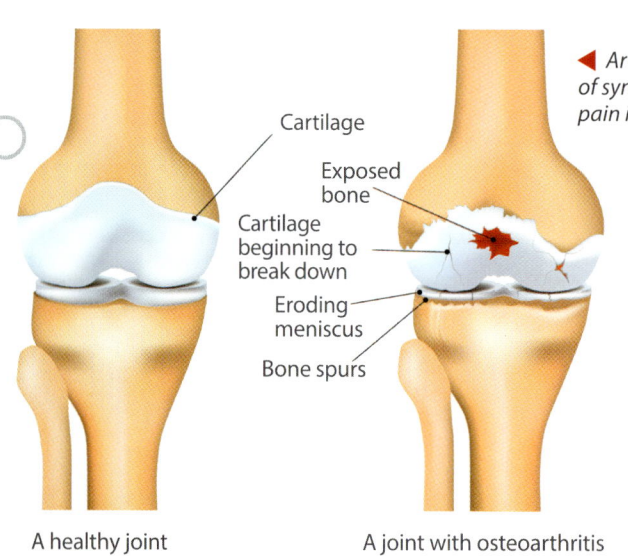

◀ Arthritis causes loss of synovial fluid, causing pain in moving joints

A healthy joint — A joint with osteoarthritis

Infectious Arthritis

Some bacteria, like staphylococcus and pneumococcus, infect the joints and cause the formation of pus. This kills cartilage cells, leading to arthritis. People who have tuberculosis and leprosy may also get arthritis, as the diseases affect their bones when they become severe. Rubella also affects the joints if the patient has not been vaccinated for it.

Rheumatoid Arthritis

This is an autoimmune disease, that is, it occurs when the immune system attacks the cells of your joints. It particularly affects the joints of the knees and elbows.

◀ Arthritis causes deformity of the hands

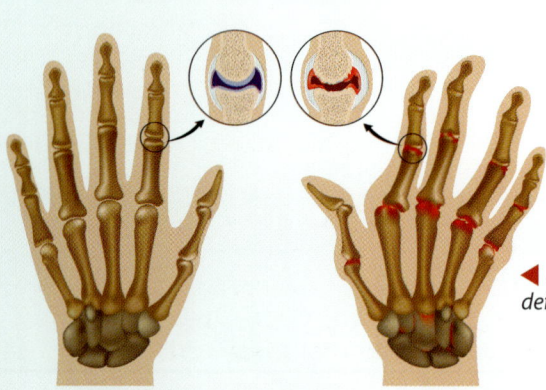

A normal hand — A hand affected by rheumatoid arthritis

HUMAN BODY — SKELETAL & MUSCULAR SYSTEM

Gout

This **bursitis**-like disease affects the knees, elbows, fingers and toes. It causes them to pain at night. This happens because uric acid crystals build up in the synovial sac.

Uric acid is a waste product of protein metabolism in the body and is removed from the blood by the kidneys. It builds up if the patient eats too much protein-rich food, drinks too little water or has kidneys that do not work properly.

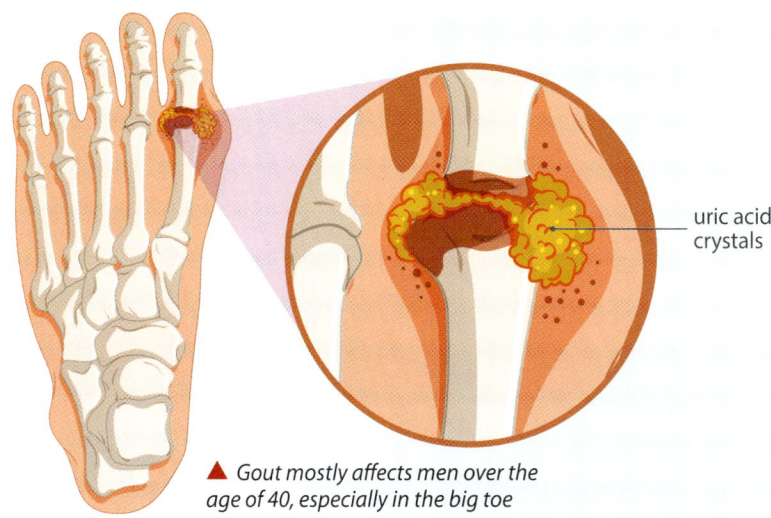

uric acid crystals

▲ *Gout mostly affects men over the age of 40, especially in the big toe*

Bursitis

Bursitis is a disease that affects the synovial bursa, tissue that connects the bones of the joint and contains the synovial fluid. It leads to a gradual deposition of insoluble calcium salts in the synovial fluid, leading to the joints becoming stiff.

Ankylosing Spondylitis

This is a disease of the vertebral column (spine). Men get it more often than women, often between the ages of 15–40. This disease causes arthritis in the joints between the vertebrae and also the joints between the vertebrae and the hip bones. Inflammation starts in the lower back and slowly moves up.

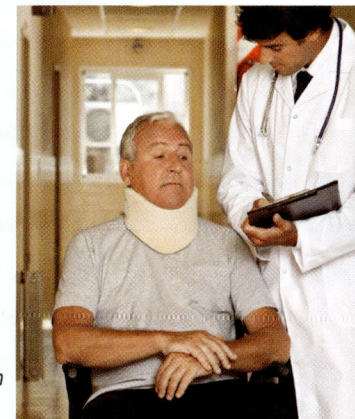

▶ *People with spondylitis often need to wear a brace to keep their neck from turning, as it can cause a lot of pain*

Rheumatic Fever

This disease is caused by bacteria called haemolytic *streptococci*. It affects the heart, nervous system and joints, causing inflammation and pain. It usually happens if a throat infection is left untreated and the bacteria are able to enter the bloodstream.

In Real Life

In the past, gout was called the 'disease of kings', since it was caused by a rich lifestyle of consuming protein-rich foods and alcoholic drinks.

Osteoporosis

As we get older, our bodies are not able to absorb enough calcium and phosphorus from food. Instead, our body makes up for what it needs by taking them from the bones. As the bones lose calcium, their structure changes and they become more sponge-like. The pores within the bones expand, making them weaker. This is called osteoporosis and makes the bones more likely to fracture in case of an accident or a fall. It also makes the spine bend over, causing a condition called hunchback. Women are more prone to developing osteoporosis.

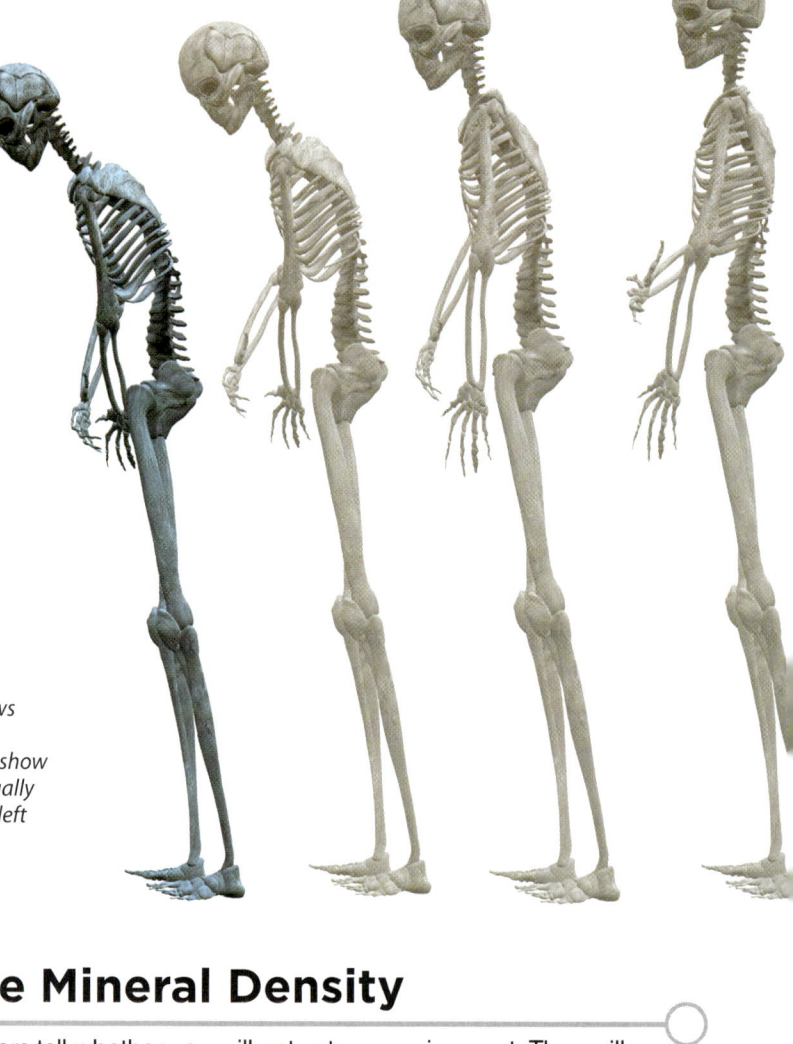

▶ The first skeleton shows a person suffering from osteoporosis. The others show how the bones are gradually weakened, from right to left

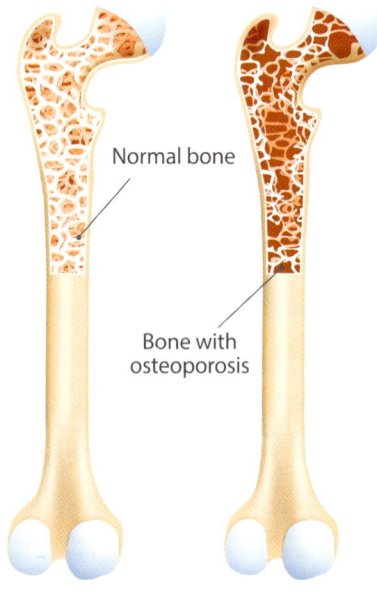

▲ Osteoporosis weakens bones, making them unable to bear the body's weight

In Real Life

Not getting enough Vitamin D in their diet causes rickets in children. Such children grow up with bent bones, a soft skull, low height and their teeth do not erupt in time.

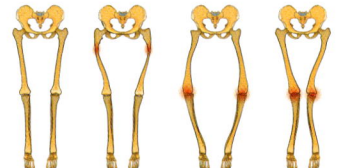

▲ The first figure shows healthy bones. The remaining three show bones affected by rickets

Bone Mineral Density

This is how doctors tell whether you will get osteoporosis or not. They will take a special X-ray called a DXA scan, which tells them the density of minerals (calcium and phosphorus) in 1 cm² of bone. They compare this with the density of other healthy people of your age and gender to get a T-score. If the T-score is −2.5, that means your bones are dangerously below the density they need to be.

What to Do about Osteoporosis

First, you need to know how you can get it. If a person does not get enough calcium from food, does not exercise enough, is underweight or smokes or drinks too much alcohol, then that person has a very high risk of getting osteoporosis. If you have dense bones to begin with, they might not become very weak. That is why men have lower chances of getting osteoporosis than women. Some kinds of cancers and intestinal disorders may also lead to osteoporosis.

This disease is hard to cure but easy to prevent. Eating food rich in calcium and Vitamin D (which helps your body absorb calcium) and taking long morning walks or jogs throughout life is good enough.

▶ Foods rich in calcium and phosphorus fight osteoporosis

Muscular Diseases

These are diseases that cause muscles to weaken. In muscular dystrophy (MD), patients show weakening of muscles, as muscular tissue is slowly replaced with fatty tissue. Patients slowly become unable to balance themselves, walk or lift their arms and also suffer from breathing and heart problems. This disease is hereditary, that is, it is because of defects in the genes you get from your parents. There are many types of MD, depending on how the disease progresses. Another disease that affects muscles is myasthenia gravis, in which your immune system attacks your muscles.

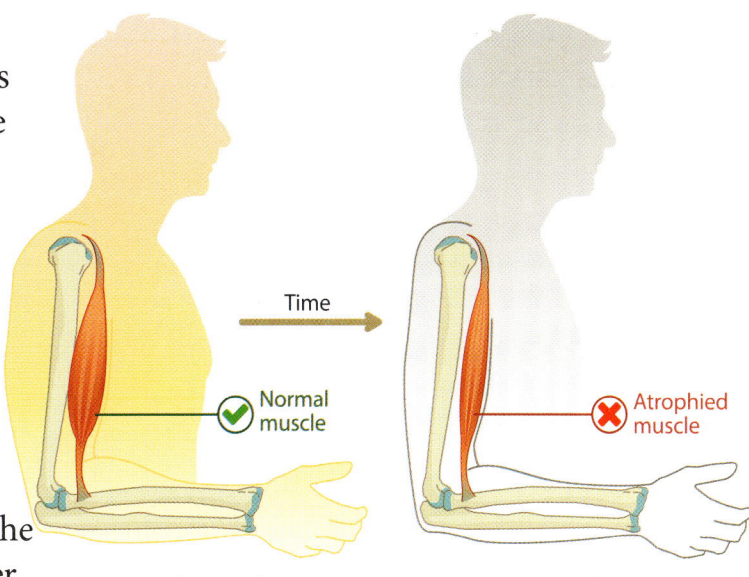

▲ Muscular dystrophy causes progressive weakness of muscles as muscle cells die off one by one

Duchenne Muscular Dystrophy (DMD)

In DMD, a gene on the X-chromosome is mutated, so that the muscles do not make dystrophin. Dystrophin is a protein that the muscles need to keep the muscle fibres bound together. Without it, muscle cells get damaged and die easily.

Because men have one X-chromosome while women have two, men who inherit the gene from their mothers will get DMD. Women do not get the disease, but there is a 50 per cent chance that they will give it to their sons. Few men who have this disease make it past the age of 20.

▶ Duchenne Muscular Dystrophy (DMD) occurs in one of every 3300 males

Myasthenia Gravis

You can get this disease if your immune system develops antibodies against acetylcholine receptors in the junction of the motor neurones and muscles. Doctors call myasthenia gravis an autoimmune disease. It causes muscles in the face, neck, throat and limbs to become weak, so patients are often unable to swallow food, or even close the mouth. It is even difficult for them to smile. Over time, muscles may weaken and die. There is no cure, but patients are given steroid drugs to suppress the immune system.

◀ Droopy eyelids and an inability to show facial expressions are symptoms of myasthenia gravis

ⓢ Incredible Individuals

'Darius Goes West' is an award-winning documentary about Darius Weems (1989–2016), a teenager with DMD, going on an 11,000-km road trip across America to raise awareness about the disease.

The movie raised over 2 million US dollars, which were given to Charley's Fund set up for DMD research. Darius gave it the $52,000 he was given in prizes.

Word Check

Aerobic respiration: It refers to the conversion of glucose to carbon dioxide.

Anaerobic respiration: It refers to the conversion of glucose to lactic acid in muscles.

Articular cartilage: It is the cartilage that cushions the bones in a joint.

Biceps brachii and triceps: They are the muscles that flex the forearm.

Bursitis: It is the infection of the synovial sac.

Cardiac muscles: It is a muscle that keeps the heart pumping.

Carpals: They are the bones of the wrist.

Collagen: It is a protein that forms threads easily. It is seen in tendons and ligaments, as well as hair and nails.

Cranial Sutures: They are the immovable joints between skull bones, except the mandible.

Endoskeleton: An overarching supportive structure or shell inside an organism.

Exoskeleton: A tough exterior structure or shell that protects an organism.

Femur: It is the thigh bone.

Fracture: It is a break in the bones caused by stress exerted upon them.

Gluteus: They are the muscles that flex the legs.

Humerus: It is the bone of the upper arm.

Intervertebral disc: It is a piece of cartilage that cushions vertebra from each other.

Joints: They are the junctions between bones. Joints may be movable or immovable.

Ligaments: They are the collagen sheets that help with the movement of the joints.

Mandible: It is the bone of the lower jaw.

Marrow: It is the fleshy tissue within bones.

Maxilla: It is the bone of the upper jaw.

Metacarpals: They are bones found in the palm of the hand.

Metatarsals: They are the bones of the sole.

Myocardium: It is the muscular part of the heart wall.

Myofibril: It is the functional unit of a muscle.

Neuromuscular junction (NMJ): It is a connection between muscles and motor neurones.

Orbit: It is the socket in the skull where the eye sits.

Osteoblasts: They are cells that make collagen.

Osteoclasts: These are the cells that resorb the bone's matrix to remodel it.

Osteoporosis: It is a disorder where a person suffers from a loss of minerals from bones, making them weak.

Pectoral girdle: It is the part of the skeleton to which the forelimbs are attached.

Pelvic girdle: The part of the skeleton to which the hindlimbs are attached.

Phalanges: They are the bones of the fingers and toes.

Radius and Ulna: They are the bones of the lower arm.

Ribs: They are the C-shaped bones in the chest.

Skull: It is the collective name for facial bones and the bones that protect the brain.

Smooth Muscle: It is a muscle that carries out involuntary movement.

Sternum: It is a tie-shaped bone in front of the chest.

Striated muscles: It is a muscle that carries out voluntary movement.

Synovial Fluid: It is the fluid that lubricates joints.

Tarsals: They are the bones of the ankle.

Tendons: It is a tissue that attaches muscle to the bone.

Thoracic basket: Also called the rib cage, it is made by the ribs, sternum and the spine, which encase the heart and lungs.

Tibia and Fibula: They are the bones of the lower leg.

Vertebra: It is a unit of the vertebral column.

Vertebral column: It is the chain of 33 bones in the back that supports the skeleton. It is also called the spine.